P9-CLU-937

# Are Judges
# Political?

CASS R. SUNSTEIN, DAVID SCHKADE,
LISA M. ELLMAN, AND ANDRES SAWICKI

# Are Judges Political?

## An Empirical Analysis
## of the Federal Judiciary

BROOKINGS INSTITUTION PRESS
*Washington, D.C.*

*Copyright © 2006*
THE BROOKINGS INSTITUTION
1775 Massachusetts Avenue, N.W., Washington, D.C. 20036
www.brookings.edu

*Library of Congress Cataloging-in-Publication data*
Are judges political? : an empirical analysis of the federal
judiciary / Cass R. Sunstein, [et al.].
    p.   cm.
  Includes index.
  ISBN-13: 978-0-8157-8234-6 (cloth : alk. paper)
  ISBN-10: 0-8157-8234-9 (cloth : alk. paper)
   1. Judges—United States.   2. Judicial process—United
States.   3. Political questions and judicial power—United
States.   I. Sunstein, Cass R.   II. Title.
  KF8775.A97 2006
  347.73'14—dc22                                  2006012477

9 8 7 6 5 4 3 2 1

The paper used in this publication meets minimum requirements of the
American National Standard for Information Sciences—Permanence of
Paper for Printed Library Materials: ANSI Z39.48-1992.

Typeset in Sabon with Linotype Didot display

Composition by R. Lynn Rivenbark
Macon, Georgia

Printed by R. R. Donnelley
Harrisonburg, Virginia

# Contents

# Preface

Americans are arguing about the future of the federal judiciary. It is an understatement to say that recent years have seen an intense battle over the federal courts—about what they are doing and why, and about whether they should be reoriented in some fundamental way.

This book does not attempt to take a stand on that battle. Our goal is much more specific. We seek to inform the debate by providing concrete information about judicial behavior. We attempt to explore, with some simple tools, the question of whether, and in what sense, appellate judges can be said to be "political." As we shall see, Republican appointees and Democratic appointees differ in their voting patterns, often very significantly. As we shall often see, there is a substantial difference, in many controversial areas, between the decisions of all-Republican panels and those of all-Democratic panels. This difference can be found in many of the most contested issues in law and politics, such as disability discrimination, abortion, campaign finance regulation, gay rights, affirmative action, sex discrimination, and environmental protection. Sometimes federal judges show a strong tendency to conformity. Sometimes they become relatively extreme.

It would be easy to read our findings to support the simple and unambivalent conclusion that federal judges are, in an important sense, political or ideological. But we do not read our findings to support that simple view. Even in the most controversial cases, the law imposes a great deal of discipline, in the sense that Republican appointees and Democratic appointees agree more often than they disagree. To be sure, it is misleading, and even foolish, to say that in hard cases, judges simply "follow the law." Some of the time, there is no law to follow. The absence of binding law is what makes hard cases hard. In such cases, the convictions of particular, flesh-and-blood judges—their own views about how to handle difficult questions—inevitably play a role. But the role of those views, once uncovered by the actual data, is far more interesting than can be captured by any simple claims about the relationship between law and politics.

We regard our work on these questions as a start and no more. The United States has an extraordinary wealth of information about judicial voting behavior, and almost all of it, though not much analyzed, is in the public domain. The information goes back many decades. With a lot of hard work, and a little creativity, it is possible to learn an enormous amount about the behavior of federal judges—and because federal judges are human, about the behavior of human beings as well. We are acutely aware that our efforts only scratch the surface of what might be done. One of our principal hopes is that we might help to spur much more work in this general vein. Such work will often replace speculation with hard facts, not only about courts as a whole, and not only about changes over time, but also about particular courts and even particular judges.

We are grateful to many people for their help with this book. Thanks go first to the dean of the University of Chicago Law School, Saul Levmore, who supported our project from an early stage. This book would not be possible without his ideas, his enthusiasm, and his help. Special thanks to the large and extraordinary team of University of Chicago law students who helped to collect the data; they include Ross Abbey, Usman Ahmed, Alyshea Austern, Raegan Barnes, Sam Bray, Caryn Campbell, Brian Downing, Ben Glatstein, Jessica Hall, Daniel Hoying, Shannon Jones, Naria Kim, Priya Laroia, Mary McKinney, Ken Merber, Cristina Miller-Ojeda, Hartley Nisenbaum, Rob Park, Annie Pogue, David Scenna, Dana Mawdsley Shank, Meghan Skirving, Franita Smith, Catherine Spector, Sarah Sulkowski,Tamer Tullgren, Asma Uddin, Shana Wallace, and Tiffany Wong. (Apologies to anyone whom we might have missed.) Abbie Willard provided excellent administrative assistance.

At various stages, we received valuable comments from many people, including Matthew Adler, Frank H. Easterbrook, Robert Hahn, Sendhil Mullainathan, Eric A. Posner, Richard A. Posner, and Richard Thaler. We are also grateful to participants in workshops at the Brookings Institution, Harvard Law School (with excellent comments from Charles Fried and Martha Minow), the University of Southern California, the University of Chicago Law School, and the University of Chicago Business School. A rationality workshop at the University of Chicago provided help at a late stage; special thanks to Gary Becker and Richard A. Posner for their excellent comments on that occasion. At a near-final stage, graduate students at Harvard's economics department offered many constructive suggestions and challenges. Warm thanks as well to Mary Kwak at the Brookings Institution for help of multiple kinds.

A preliminary version of some of the findings and analysis in this book appeared in Cass R. Sunstein, David Schkade, and Lisa M. Ellman, "Ideological Voting in Federal Courts of Appeals: A Preliminary Analysis," 90 *Virginia Law Review* 301 (2004); we are most grateful to the editors of the *Virginia Law Review* for their assistance.

We are thankful, finally, to the numerous federal judges who expressed interest in our project and who offered us exceedingly valuable comments—sometimes enthusiastic, always clarifying and instructive, occasionally skeptical. The United States is blessed with a federal judiciary characterized by its integrity, its excellence, and its unwavering commitment to the law. For all the complexity of our findings, we conclude our project with even greater faith in both the quality and the character of the nation's federal judges.

# Are Judges
# Political?

# Studying Judges with Numbers | 1

In the last two decades, the United States has witnessed some exceedingly heated debates about the composition of the federal judiciary. Are judges "activists"? Should they stop "legislating from the bench"? Are they abusing their authority? Or are they protecting fundamental rights in a way that is indispensable in a free society? What, exactly, are they doing, and what should they do differently?

Several American presidents have sought to populate the federal courts with judges who, it was hoped, were likely to rule in their preferred directions. In issues including abortion, separation of church and state, environmental protection, and criminals' rights, presidents have wanted judges of a particular kind. On occasion, the United States Senate has checked the president by blocking nominees who were expected to rule in ways that senators disapproved. Under President Bill Clinton, for example, the Republican-controlled Senate Committee on the Judiciary refused to schedule hearings on a number of nominees, effectively preventing their confirmation. To some Republicans, President Clinton's nominees were simply too "liberal." Under President George W. Bush, a Democratic minority in the Senate succeeded in filibustering several controversial nominees. To some Democrats, President Bush's nominees were simply too "conservative." In 2005 Republican and Democratic senators reached an agreement by which most of President Bush's controversial nominees would be confirmed—but the filibuster has yet to be taken off the table.

The objection to presidential nominees to the federal bench has, of course, been most fierce during debates over the Supreme Court. In 1987 President Ronald Reagan's nomination of an extremely distinguished appellate judge, Robert Bork, was rejected by the Senate by a vote of 58 to 42. The rejection was largely based on ideological grounds; no one argued that Judge Bork was incompetent, and the real concern, to his critics, was his likely pattern of votes. President Clinton's choice of Supreme Court nominees was constrained by the anticipated reactions of Republican senators. His ultimate choices, Ruth Bader Ginsburg and Stephen Breyer, were "precleared," in the sense that prominent Republicans signaled that they would be acceptable.

In his own decisions about Supreme Court nominees, President George W. Bush has been entirely aware of the possible negative votes of Democratic senators. His first nominee, John Roberts, was widely regarded as superb in quality and also as acceptable, on ideological grounds, to many moderates and liberals. President Bush's second nominee, White House Counsel Harriet Miers, withdrew after a series of complaints about her lack of experience and about what some conservatives considered to be her insufficiently conservative record. Samuel Alito, President Bush's third nominee, attracted considerable controversy. While no one doubted his credentials, a number of Democrats objected that he was simply too conservative—unduly respectful of executive power and unlikely to safeguard individual rights. Nonetheless, Justice Alito was confirmed by a vote of 58 to 42.

But the focus on the Supreme Court should not obscure the immense importance of lower court nominees. The decisions of lower courts are rarely reviewed by the Supreme Court; their decisions are effectively final. As a result, the courts of appeals play an exceedingly large role both in settling disputes and determining the likely direction of the law. It is for this reason that the likely votes of lower court nominees have played a significant role in national debates.

Underneath these political contests is a degree of uncertainty about how judges actually behave. What is the relationship between judicial votes and political convictions? Is it sensible to divide judges into "liberals" and "conservatives"? Or is it better to say that judges generally follow the law, in a way that makes political views irrelevant? Might the answer to both of the last two questions be a firm no?

## Judges and Presidents

The major goal of this book is to shed new light on these questions, simply by looking at what judges actually do.[1] Our focus is insistently empirical. We have compiled a large and distinctive data set, consisting of many thousands of judicial votes in numerous domains. We aim to analyze the data to answer some unresolved questions about the federal judiciary. Almost all of our focus is on the courts of appeals, which are uniquely easy, and uniquely informative, to study. For our purposes, a particular virtue of the federal courts is their intermediate character. The Supreme Court resolves the most difficult and contested cases, and hence it is not exactly a surprise if Republican appointees vote differently from Democratic appointees. The federal district courts conduct trials, and many of their cases are routine, at least as a matter of law; it should not be surprising if, in such cases, Republican and Democratic appointees are essentially indistinguishable. (We are not claiming that this is in fact the case in all domains.) The courts of appeals decide cases that are often difficult and contested, but usually not so much so as those that reach the Supreme Court. The decisions of these courts therefore provide an exceedingly illuminating test of the role of politics in judicial judgments.

With respect to federal courts of appeals, the United States has, in fact, been conducting an extraordinary and longstanding natural experiment. The experiment involves the relationship between presidential choices and judicial decisions. The vast majority of appellate decisions are rendered by three-judge panels, and the membership of these panels is the result of a random draw from the group of judges sitting on the circuit in which the case is appealed. Because of the random assignment of judges, it is possible to study how Republican and Democratic appointees differ from one another in a remarkably wide range of cases. If presidents care about a judge's likely rulings—and what president does not?—then an investigation of the effect of presidential appointments will tell us something important. Most simply, it will show whether Republican and Democratic presidents select judges with different views, and it will show the extent to which they differ as well. Such an investigation will also provide some information on the relationship between what might be called "political ideology" and judicial judgments.

To be sure, many people believe that, as a general rule, political ideology should not and does not affect legal judgments. We agree, and we shall attempt to show that this belief contains some important truth.[2] Frequently the law is clear, and judges should and will simply implement it, no matter who has appointed them. Both President George W. Bush and Senator John Kerry, for example, have emphasized that judges ought to follow the law, and we shall provide considerable evidence to suggest that they do exactly that. But what happens when the law is unclear? In that event, it is hopelessly inadequate to ask judges to "follow the law." By hypothesis, the law does not provide anything to "follow." In such cases, does the political affiliation of the appointing president matter? What role does ideology play then?

It is easy to imagine two quite different positions. It might be predicted that even when the law is unclear, in the sense that binding precedents cannot be found, ideology does not matter; the legal culture itself imposes a sharp discipline on judges, so that judges vote as judges rather than as ideologues. Perhaps judges protect freedom of speech, or equality under the law, regardless of their personal beliefs, even in difficult cases not controlled by existing law. Alternatively, it might be predicted that, in hard cases, the judges' "attitudes" end up predicting their votes, so that liberal judges, or judges appointed by Democratic presidents, show systematically different votes from those of conservative judges, or those appointed by Republican presidents. The "attitudinal model," influential and well known in law and politics, attempts to explain judicial votes in just these terms.[3]

It is important to make a distinction here. We might want to test the effects of the political affiliation of the appointing president; alternatively, we might want to test the effects of judicial ideology itself. It would be exceedingly valuable to know whether and where Republican appointees differ from Democratic appointees. It would also be valuable to know the differences across presidents. For example, do the appointees of President Bill Clinton differ from those of President Jimmy Carter? What are the differences, if any, among the appointees of Presidents Richard Nixon, Ronald Reagan, George H. W. Bush, and George W. Bush?

We are able to make considerable progress on these questions, and hence we shall focus throughout the book on the political affiliation of the appointing president. But that affiliation is only a proxy for judicial ideology. Democratic presidents have been known to appoint relatively conservative judges, and Republican presidents have been known to appoint relatively liberal ones.[4] In American history, many presidents have followed the practice of "senatorial courtesy," by which senators from the president's party have a substantial role in picking judges to fill seats in their own states.[5] As a result, there can be a significant difference between a president's political commitments and the general approach of the judges appointed by that president.

This point should not be overstated. In the modern era, at least, presidents are usually interested in ensuring that judicial appointees are of a certain stripe. A Democratic president is unlikely to want to appoint judges who will seek to overrule *Roe v. Wade*[6] and strike down affirmative action programs. A Republican president is unlikely to want to appoint judges who will interpret the Constitution to require states to recognize same-sex marriages or to eliminate religion from the public sphere. It is reasonable to hypothesize that as a statistical regularity, judges appointed by Republican presidents (hereinafter described, for ease of exposition, as Republican appointees) will be more conservative than judges appointed by Democratic presidents (Democratic appointees, as we shall henceforth call them).

But is this hypothesis true? If so, when is it true, and to what degree is it true? What exactly is meant, in this context, by "more conservative"? We shall try to answer these questions. In a way, the political affiliation of the appointing president actually provides a more interesting benchmark than ideology itself, assuming that we could obtain direct access to it (as some studies have done, in efforts to explore the role of judicial ideology as such).[7] Does it matter whether judges are appointed by a Democratic or a Republican president? If so, when does it matter, and how much does it matter? What difference do particular presidents make? Were President Reagan's appointees, for example, different from President Nixon's appointees?

There is a more subtle and more intriguing possibility. Human beings are often influenced by other human beings, particularly those with whom they frequently interact. When like-minded people get together, they often go to extremes.[8] And sometimes people suppress their private views and conform to the apparent views of others. Drawing on these findings, we might speculate that federal appellate judges are subject to "panel effects"—that the votes of individual judges are affected by the votes of other judges on the panel. On a three-judge panel, a judge's likely vote might well be affected by the other two judges assigned to the same panel. In particular, we might ask: *Does a judge vote differently depending on whether she is sitting with no judge, one judge, or two judges appointed by a president of the same political party?*

It might be hypothesized that a Republican appointee, sitting with two Democratic appointees, would be more likely to vote as Democratic appointees typically do—whereas a Democratic appointee, sitting with two Republican appointees, would be more likely to vote as Republican appointees typically do. But is this, in fact, the usual pattern? Is it an invariable one? Recall that judges in a given circuit are assigned to panels (and, therefore, to cases) randomly. A fortunate consequence is that the existence of a large data set allows these issues to be investigated empirically.[9]

## Controversial Cases and Three Hypotheses

In this book, we examine many different areas of the law, focusing on a number of controversial issues that seem especially likely to reveal divisions between Republican and Democratic appointees. Our list of areas is long. We explore cases involving abortion, affirmative action, campaign finance, capital punishment, Commerce Clause challenges to congressional enactments, commercial speech, congressional abrogation of state sovereign immunity, the Contracts Clause, criminal appeals, disability discrimination, the Federal Communications Commission (FCC), gay and lesbian rights, environmental regulation, the National Labor Relations Board (NLRB), the National Environmental Policy Act[10] (NEPA), obscenity, standing, school and racial segregation, piercing the corporate veil, punitive damages, race discrimination, sex discrimination, sexual harassment, and takings of private property without just compensation. We will offer a more detailed description of our subjects and methods below.

Our initial goal is to examine three hypotheses:

1. *Ideological voting.* In ideologically contested cases, involving the most controversial issues of the day, a judge's ideological tendency can be predicted by the party of the appointing president: Republican appointees vote very differently from Democratic appointees.

2. *Ideological dampening.* A judge's ideological tendency is likely to be dampened if she is sitting with two judges of a different political party. For example, a Democratic appointee should be less likely to vote in a stereotypically liberal fashion if accompanied by two Republican appointees, and a Republican appointee should be less likely to vote in a stereotypically conservative fashion if accompanied by two Democratic appointees. If ideological dampening occurs, it follows that in disability dis-

crimination cases, Democratic appointees will be more likely to side with employers when sitting with two Republican appointees—and that when sitting with two Democratic appointees, Republican appointees will be more likely to side with disabled people.

3. *Ideological amplification.* A judge's ideological tendency, in ideologically contested cases, is likely to be amplified if she is sitting with two judges from the same political party. A Democratic appointee should show an increased tendency to vote in a stereotypically liberal fashion if accompanied by two Democratic appointees, and a Republican appointee should be more likely to vote in a stereotypically conservative fashion if accompanied by two Republican appointees. If this hypothesis turns out to be true, it would have large implications, because it would suggest that like-minded judges might well go to extremes.

Note that for purposes of measuring ideological dampening and ideological amplification, we take, as the baseline for analysis, cases in which a judge sits with one Republican appointee and one Democratic appointee. Unfortunately, we do not have any record of how federal judges vote in isolation. But it seems natural, and at least illuminating, to start with cases in which judges sit with an appointee of both parties, and to see how their patterns shift when they sit with two appointees of a single party.

We find that in numerous areas of the law, all three hypotheses are strongly confirmed.[11] Each hypothesis finds support in federal cases involving affirmative action, NEPA challenges, congressional abrogation of state sovereign immunity, sex discrimination, disability discrimination, sexual harassment, review of environmental regulations, campaign finance, piercing the corporate veil, racial discrimination, segregation, obscenity, Contracts Clause violations, restrictions on commercial advertising, and the NLRB. In such cases, our aggregate data support all three hypotheses.

Indeed, we find many extreme cases of ideological dampening, which we might call "leveling effects," in which party differences are wiped out by the influence of panel composition. When leveling effects are present, Democratic appointees, when sitting with two Republican appointees, are at least as likely to vote in the stereotypically conservative fashion as are Republican appointees when sitting with two Democratic appointees. In fact, we find many areas in which Democratic appointees sitting with two Republicans show *more* conservative voting patterns than do Republicans sitting with two Democratic appointees. The same shift can be shown for Republican appointees as well.

Perhaps most important, we also find strong amplification effects, in which judges show far more ideological voting patterns when they are sitting with two judges appointed by a president of the same political party. Amplification effects are so strong that if the data set in the relevant cases is taken as a whole, Democratic appointees sitting with two Democratic appointees are about *twice* as likely to vote in the stereotypically liberal fashion as are Republican appointees sitting with two Republican appointees. This is a far larger disparity than the disparity between Democratic and Republican votes when either is sitting with one Democratic appointee and one Republican appointee.

In most of the areas investigated here, the political party of the appointing president is a fairly good predictor of how individual judges will vote. Hence the affiliation of the appointing president matters a great deal to the content of the law. But in those same areas, the political party of the presidents who appointed the other two judges on the panel is at least as good a predictor of how individual judges will vote! If you would like to know how a particular judge is likely to vote in a controversial area of the law, you will often do well to ask: What is the political affiliation of the president who appointed the two other judges on the panel? All in all, Democratic appointees show somewhat greater susceptibility to panel effects than do Republican appointees. What this means is that Democratic appointees are more vulnerable to the views of their fellow judges, and hence more likely to show both dampening and amplification.

But there are noteworthy counterexamples to our general findings. In five important areas, ideology does not predict judicial votes, and hence all three hypotheses are refuted. This is the pattern in cases involving criminal appeals, takings claims, challenges to punitive damages awards, standing to sue, and Commerce Clause challenges to congressional enactments. In two other areas, the first hypothesis is supported, but the second and third hypotheses are refuted, and hence ideological voting is unaccompanied by panel effects. These areas—the only ones in which judges are unaffected by other judges—are abortion and capital punishment. In both of these areas, judges apparently vote their convictions at a consistent rate and are not influenced by panel composition. The area of gay and lesbian rights similarly shows ideological voting without dampening or amplification—but because of the small sample size, we can say only that the second and third hypotheses are neither supported nor refuted.

We offer a number of other findings. We show that variations in panel composition lead to dramatically different outcomes, in a way that creates serious problems for the rule of law. In the cases we analyze, a panel composed of three Democratic appointees issues a liberal ruling 62 percent of the time, whereas a panel composed of three Republican appointees issues a liberal ruling only 36 percent of the time. The difference of 26 percent is strikingly large. Not surprisingly, mixed panels show intermediate figures. A panel composed of two Republican appointees and one Democrat issues a liberal ruling 41 percent of the time; a panel composed of two Democratic appointees and one Republican does so 52 percent of the time.

These differences should not be overread. Despite their size, they certainly do not show that the likely result is foreordained by the composition of the panel. There is a substantial overlap between the votes of Republican appointees and those of Democratic appointees. The political affiliation of the appointing president is hardly everything. But there can be no doubt that the litigant's chances, in the cases we examine, are significantly affected by the luck of the draw.

To understand the importance of group dynamics on judicial panels, it is important to emphasize that a Democratic majority, or a Republican majority, has enough votes to do what it wishes. Apparently, however, a large disciplining effect comes from the presence of a single panelist from another party. Hence all-Republican panels show far more conservative patterns than majority Republican panels, and all-Democratic panels show far more liberal patterns than majority Democratic panels.

Our tale is largely one of effects from the political affiliation of the appointing president on individual voting and panel outcomes. But the tale is not unqualified. As noted, we find several areas in which the appointing president does not matter at all—even though the pool of cases studied here is limited to domains where it would be expected to play a large role. Outside of many of the domains we study, Republican and Democratic appointees are far less likely to differ. The absence of party effects in important and contested areas (for example, criminal appeals, takings, punitive damages, standing to sue, and Commerce Clause challenges) testifies to the possibility of commonalities across partisan lines, even when differences might be expected. And where party differences are statistically significant, they are usually not huge.

Note that in the entire sample, Democratic appointees issue a liberal vote 52 percent of the time, whereas Republicans do so 40 percent of the time. The full story emphasizes the significant effects of ideology and also the limited nature of those effects. We shall spend considerable time on the complexities here.

Among lawyers and law professors, there is also a great deal of speculation about whether some of the circuit courts, in some parts of the country, are more conservative than others. Disaggregating our data, we also provide evidence of how ideology varies by circuit, showing that by a simple measure, the Ninth, Third, and Second Circuits are the most liberal, while the Seventh, Eighth, and First are the most conservative. In terms of basic patterns, we find striking similarities across circuits. In *all* circuits, Democratic appointees are more likely than Republican appointees to vote in a stereotypically liberal direction. At the same time, however, a judge's vote is generally no better predicted by his or her own party than it is by the party of the other two judges on the panel.

We shall also investigate changes across time. Are courts becoming more liberal or more conservative? Is there a difference between the judicial appointees of President Reagan and President George W. Bush? What might be said about the appointees of President Clinton? What difference does a "big" decision, such as *Roe* v. *Wade*, make to judicial voting patterns over time? We shall give some reason to think that the federal courts are indeed becoming more conservative—and that there is no significant ideological difference among the appointees of Presidents Reagan, George H. W. Bush, and George W. Bush. But these questions are especially difficult to investigate, because the mix of cases changes over time, with the emergence of new areas of the law and with strategic decisions by prospective litigants about when to sue and when to settle.

## Explanations and Implications

Our main goal is simply to present and analyze the data—and to show the extent to which the three central hypotheses, and several others, find vindication. But we also aim to give some explanation for our findings and to relate them to some continuing debates about the role of ideology on federal panels. Our data do not reveal whether ideological dampening is a product of persuasion or instead a form of collegiality. If Republican appointees show a liberal pattern of votes when accompanied by two Democratic appointees, it might be because they are convinced by their colleagues. Alternatively, they might suppress their private doubts and accept the majority's view. It is also possible that they are able to affect the reasoning in the majority opinion, trading their vote in return for a more moderate statement of the law.

In any case, it is reasonable to say that the data show the pervasiveness of what we shall call the "collegial concurrence": a concurrence by a judge who signs the panel's opinion either because he is persuaded by the shared opinion of the two other judges on the panel or because it is not worthwhile, all things considered, to dissent. The collegial concurrence can be taken as an example, in the unlikely setting of judicial panels, of responsiveness to conformity pressures.[12] Such pressures make it more likely that people will end up silencing themselves, or even publicly agreeing with a majority position, simply because they would otherwise be isolated in their disagreement. We will discuss these issues at greater length after presenting the data.

We also find evidence within the federal judiciary of *group polarization*, by which like-minded people move toward a more extreme position in the same direction as their predeliberation views.[13] If all-Republican panels are overwhelmingly likely to strike down campaign finance regulation, and if all-Democratic panels are overwhelmingly likely to uphold affirmative action programs, group polarization is likely to be a reason. Finally, we offer indirect evidence of a "whistleblower effect": A single judge of another party, while likely to be affected by the fact that he is isolated, might also influence other judges on the panel, at least where the panel would otherwise fail to follow existing law.[14]

We believe that our findings are of considerable interest in themselves, simply because they tell us a great deal about judicial behavior. We think that the findings also reveal something about human behavior in many contexts. A wide range of social science evidence shows conformity effects: When people are confronted with the views of unanimous others, they tend to yield.[15] Sometimes they yield because they believe that unanimous others cannot be wrong; sometimes they yield because it is not worthwhile to dissent in public.[16] In showing a tendency to conform, federal judges appear to act like other human beings do.

As we have mentioned, a great deal of social science evidence shows that like-minded people tend to go to extremes.[17] In the real world, this hypothesis is extremely hard to test in light of the range of confounding variables. But our data provide strong evidence that like-minded judges also go to extremes: The probability that a judge will vote in one or another direction is greatly increased by the presence of judges appointed by the president of the same political party. In short, we claim to show both strong conformity effects and group polarization within federal courts of appeals. If these effects can be shown there, then they are also likely to be found in many other diverse contexts.

In fact, the presence of such effects both supports and complicates what is probably the most influential method for explaining judicial voting: the "attitudinal model,"[18] to which we have previously referred. According to the attitudinal model, judges have certain "attitudes" toward areas of the law, and these attitudes are good predictors of judicial votes in difficult cases.[19] Insofar as party effects are present, our findings are highly supportive of this idea; in many areas, we provide fresh support for the attitudinal model. But that model does not come fully to terms with panel effects, which can both dampen and amplify the tendencies to which judicial "attitudes" give rise. Since panel effects are generally as large as party effects, and sometimes even larger, the attitudinal model misses a crucial factor behind judicial votes.

A disclaimer: The federal reporters offer an astonishingly large data set of judicial votes, including over two hundred years of votes ranging over countless substantive areas. Our own investigation is limited to areas that, by general agreement, are ideologically contested—enough to produce possible disagreements in the cases that find their way to the courts of appeals.[20] We have only scratched the surface. Of course, it would be extremely interesting to know much more.[21] Might ideological voting and panel effects be found in apparently nonideological cases involving, for example, bankruptcy, torts, and civil procedure? How do the three hypotheses fare in the early part of the twentieth century, when federal courts were confronting the regulatory state for the first time? In cases involving minimum wage and maximum hour laws, did Republican appointees differ from Democratic appointees, and were panel effects also significant?

In the future, it should be possible to use the techniques discussed here to test a wide range of hypotheses about judicial voting patterns. One of our central goals is to provide a method for future analysis, a method that can be used in countless contexts. With suitable adaptations, the data that we have examined can also shed light on many other questions, including the ideological orientations of particular judges, not merely of large sets of appointees.

# Ideological Votes and Ideological Panels  2

W̱e examined a total of 6,408 published three-judge panel decisions and the 19,224 associated votes of individual judges.[1] The cases involved abortion,[2] capital punishment,[3] the Americans with Disabilities Act (ADA),[4] criminal appeals,[5] takings,[6] the Contracts Clause,[7] affirmative action,[8] racial discrimination cases brought by African American plaintiffs under Title VII of the Civil Rights Act of 1964,[9] sex discrimination,[10] campaign finance,[11] sexual harassment,[12] cases in which plaintiffs sought to pierce the corporate veil,[13] the National Environmental Policy Act (NEPA),[14] gay and lesbian rights,[15] congressional abrogation of state sovereign immunity,[16] First Amendment challenges to commercial advertising restrictions,[17] challenges to punitive damage awards,[18] constitutional and statutory challenges to obscenity rulings,[19] challenges to environmental regulations,[20] challenges to Federal Communication Commission (FCC) rulings,[21] challenges to National Labor Relations Board (NLRB) rulings,[22] racial segregation cases,[23] standing to bring suit in federal court,[24] and federalism challenges to congressional enactments under the Commerce Clause.[25]

Our methods for finding and assessing these cases, described in the footnotes, leave room for errors and sometimes for a degree of discretion. We are confident, however, that we have accurately identified the basic patterns of judicial votes. To keep the inquiry manageable, our investigation is often limited to recent time periods—sometimes from 1995 to 2004, though occasionally longer when necessary to produce a sufficient number of cases in a particular category.[26] It is not at all clear that similar patterns would be found in earlier periods, when splits between Democratic and Republican appointees were almost certainly much smaller. We believe that incomplete though the evidence is, our results are sufficient to show the range of likely patterns and also to establish the claim that the three principal hypotheses are often vindicated, at least in recent years.

Our sample is limited to published opinions. This limitation obviously simplifies research, but it does raise some legitimate questions. In some courts of appeals, unpublished opinions are widely believed to be simple and straightforward and not to involve difficult or complex issues of law. In such courts, it is harmless to ignore unpublished opinions, simply because they are easy. But publication practices are variable across circuits, and some unpublished opinions do involve serious and hard questions; hence the decision to focus on published cases complicates cross-circuit comparisons. Ideally, we would investigate all cases, not simply published ones, and even compare published and unpublished cases on various dimensions. But our limited focus does enable us to test our hypotheses in most of the areas that particularly interest us (and the public), while also producing at least considerable information about the role of party and panel effects across circuits.

Table 2-1 shows the percentage of stereotypically liberal votes[27] in a variety of areas. By "stereotypically liberal votes," we mean to identify a simple, crude measure, and we do not venture anything especially controversial. For example, a vote counts as stereotypically liberal if it favors a plaintiff who is complaining of discrimination on the basis of race, sex, or disability; if it upholds an affirmative action program or a campaign finance regulation; if it holds corporate officers liable for the misdeeds of their corporation; if it strikes down a restriction on sexually explicit speech; or if it upholds an environmental regulation, or a decision protecting a labor union, against industry challenge. Of course, these measures are too crude to capture all of what it means to be "liberal" or "conservative." But because of the sheer number of cases and votes, the simplicity of the measures can be counted as a virtue, enabling us to produce informative comparisons.

It is entirely to be expected that Republican appointees will often offer stereotypically liberal votes, if only because that is what the law often requires. So, too, Democratic appointees will often vote in stereotypically conservative directions because the law so mandates. Nor are Republican or Democratic appointees monolithic; no one doubts that some Republican appointees are more liberal than some Democratic appointees. The crudeness of our test is a virtue here as well. If that crude test reveals a significant overall difference between Republican and Democratic appointees—as there generally is—we will learn something important about judicial behavior.

Table 2-1 reveals both individual votes and majority decisions of three-judge panels. Note first that in a number of areas, there is strong evidence of ideological voting in the sense that Democratic appointees are far more likely to vote in the stereotypically liberal direction than are Republican appointees. We measure ideological voting by subtracting the percentage of liberal Republican votes

Table 2-1. *Summary of Votes by Individual Judges and Majority Decisions of Three-Judge Panels*[a]

| | Individual judge's votes | | | | | | | Panel majority decisions | | | | |
| | Party | | | Panel colleagues | | | | Panel composition | | | | |
| Case type | R | D | D-R | RR | RD | DD | DD-RR | RRR | RRD | DDR | DDD | DDD-RRR |
|---|---|---|---|---|---|---|---|---|---|---|---|---|
| Gay and lesbian rights (vote for plaintiff) | .16 | .57 | .40 | .27 | .23 | .60 | .33 | .14 | .22 | .25 | 1.00 | .86 |
| Affirmative action (vote for plan) | .47 | .75 | .28 | .46 | .62 | .74 | .28 | .34 | .47 | .85 | .83 | .49 |
| National Environmental Policy Act (vote for plaintiff) | .20 | .43 | .24 | .15 | .25 | .58 | .43 | .20 | .10 | .42 | .71 | .51 |
| Capital punishment (vote for defendant) | .21 | .45 | .24 | .26 | .35 | .29 | .03 | .13 | .27 | .44 | .33 | .20 |
| 11th Amendment abrogation (vote to uphold) | .38 | .59 | .21 | .38 | .50 | .58 | .20 | .27 | .48 | .50 | .70 | .43 |
| National Labor Relations Board (vote for public interest or against industry) | .37 | .57 | .20 | .33 | .48 | .62 | .28 | .25 | .43 | .55 | .75 | .50 |
| Sex discrimination (vote for plaintiff) | .35 | .52 | .17 | .35 | .42 | .58 | .23 | .30 | .37 | .50 | .76 | .46 |
| Americans with Disabilities Act (vote for plaintiff) | .27 | .43 | .16 | .25 | .36 | .43 | .19 | .17 | .29 | .44 | .50 | .33 |
| Abortion (vote pro-choice) | .51 | .67 | .16 | .61 | .56 | .63 | .01 | .60 | .51 | .66 | .71 | .11 |
| Campaign finance (vote to uphold) | .30 | .44 | .14 | .32 | .32 | .50 | .18 | .31 | .26 | .37 | .62 | .31 |

| | | | | | | | | | | | |
|---|---|---|---|---|---|---|---|---|---|---|---|
| Piercing corporate veil (vote to pierce) | .25 | .39 | .13 | .25 | .30 | .47 | .22 | .21 | .26 | .34 | .60 | .39 |
| Environmental Protection Agency (vote for public interest or against industry) | .51 | .61 | .10 | .47 | .56 | .66 | .19 | .39 | .54 | .56 | .72 | .33 |
| Obscenity (finding no violation) | .27 | .36 | .09 | .26 | .31 | .37 | .11 | .21 | .32 | .31 | .46 | .25 |
| Title VII (vote for plaintiff) | .34 | .43 | .09 | .37 | .37 | .41 | .04 | .39 | .31 | .46 | .56 | .17 |
| Desegregation (vote to desegregate) | .65 | .74 | .09 | .64 | .71 | .71 | .08 | .58 | .69 | .81 | .72 | .15 |
| Federal Communications Commission (vote for public interest or against industry) | .51 | .59 | .08 | .52 | .51 | .70 | .18 | .55 | .42 | .63 | .80 | .25 |
| Contracts (reject constitutional challenge) | .25 | .31 | .07 | .20 | .29 | .42 | .22 | .17 | .29 | .33 | .50 | .33 |
| First Amendment (finding restriction constitutional) | .53 | .59 | .06 | .52 | .56 | .60 | .08 | .43 | .54 | .69 | .50 | .07 |
| Standing (vote for standing) | .44 | .49 | .05 | .48 | .43 | .49 | .01 | .47 | .40 | .46 | .60 | .13 |
| Criminal appeals (vote for defendant) | .31 | .35 | .04 | .33 | .33 | .33 | .01 | .30 | .31 | .37 | .32 | .02 |
| Takings (find no taking) | .77 | .80 | .04 | .77 | .79 | .77 | .00 | .76 | .80 | .79 | .74 | -.02 |
| Federalism (vote to uphold) | .94 | .97 | .03 | .96 | .95 | .95 | -.02 | .96 | .98 | .96 | .97 | .01 |
| Punitive damages (upholding damages) | .74 | .73 | .00 | .74 | .76 | .65 | -.09 | .70 | .75 | .74 | .60 | -.10 |
| Average across all case types | .40 | .52 | .12 | .40 | .45 | .53 | .13 | .36 | .41 | .52 | .62 | .26 |
| Case types with a panel difference | .37 | .51 | .15 | .36 | .43 | .55 | .18 | .31 | .38 | .51 | .66 | .34 |

a. Proportion voting for the liberal position on the given issue.

from the percentage of liberal Democratic votes; the larger the number, the larger the party effect. The overall difference is 12 percent—not huge, but substantial. The extent of this effect, and even its existence, is highly variable across areas. We shall discuss these variations shortly.

We can also see that the votes of judges are significantly influenced by the party affiliation of the president who appointed the other two judges on the same panel.[28] As a first approximation, we measure this influence by subtracting the overall percentage of liberal votes by a judge of either party when sitting with two Democratic appointees from the percentage when he or she sits with two Republican appointees. Surprisingly, this overall difference, 13 percent, is even larger than the basic difference between parties. This is our simple measure of panel effects, though it is part of a more complex story. As we shall see, there are multiple ways to assess the influence of the other judges on the panel.

Finally, it is clear that these two influences result in actual judicial decisions that are very much affected by the composition of the panel. Judicial decisions are, of course, what most matter to both the litigants and the law, and hence this finding may well be the most important one. The clearest point is a sharp spread between the average outcome in an all-Republican panel and that in an all-Democratic panel. Indeed, *the likelihood of a liberal outcome is roughly twice as high with the latter as with the former.* For litigants in highly controversial areas, a great deal depends on the luck of the draw—the outcome of the assignment of judges, which is random.

Figure 2-1 captures the aggregate party and panel effects across those areas in which there is ideological voting.[29] The most striking lessons of this figure are among our principal themes here.[30] For both Democratic appointees and Republican appointees, the likelihood of a liberal vote jumps when the two other panel mem-

Figure 2-1. *Party and Panel Influences on Votes of Individual Judges*[a]

Percent liberal votes

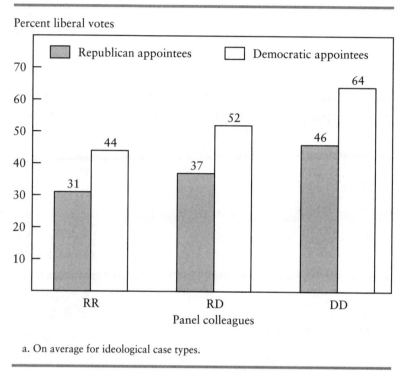

Panel colleagues

a. On average for ideological case types.

bers are Democratic appointees—and it drops when the two other panel members are Republican appointees.

Recall that for purposes of analysis, we are taking, as the baseline, cases in which a judge is sitting with one Democrat and one Republican, and we are examining how voting patterns shift when a judge is sitting instead with two Democratic appointees or two Republican appointees. We can readily see that a Democrat, in the baseline condition, casts a liberal vote 52 percent of the time, whereas a Republican does so 37 percent of the time. Sitting with two Democratic appointees, Democratic appointees cast liberal votes 64 percent of the time (an increase of 12 percent over baseline), whereas Republican appointees do so 46 percent of the time (an increase of 9 percent over baseline). Sitting with two Republican appointees, Democratic appointees cast liberal votes 44 percent of the time (a decrease of 8 percent), whereas Republican appointees do so only 31 percent of the time (a decrease of 6 percent). Thus, Republican appointees sitting with two Democratic appointees show the same basic pattern of votes (46 percent liberal votes) as do Democratic appointees sitting with two Republican appointees (44 percent liberal votes).

## All Hypotheses Supported

The aggregate figures conceal some significant differences across case categories. We begin with cases in which all three hypotheses are supported. We order the areas by the size of the party difference, starting with cases in which that difference is largest (see figure 2-2).

### Affirmative Action

Affirmative action shows the same basic pattern of results as the aggregate data, but with an unusually large overall party difference.[31] The legal question in these cases, sharply disputed within the Supreme Court, is whether and when the Constitution forbids race-conscious programs nominally intended to benefit members of racial minority groups. From 1978 through 2004, Republican appointees cast 275 total votes, with 129, or 47 percent, in favor of upholding an affirmative action program. By contrast, Democratic appointees cast 208 votes, with 156, or 75 percent, in favor of upholding an affirmative action program. Here, we find striking evidence of ideological voting.

We also find significant evidence of panel effects. An isolated Democrat sitting with two Republican appointees votes in favor of affirmative action only 60 percent of the time—approximately halfway between the aggregate numbers for Democratic appointees and Republican appointees. More remarkably, isolated Democratic appointees are actually less likely to vote for affirmative action programs than are isolated Republican appointees, who vote in favor 69 percent of the time. Thus, we see strong evidence of ideological dampening.

The third hypothesis is also confirmed. On all-Republican panels, individual Republican appointees vote for affirmative action programs only 34 percent of the time. On all-Democratic panels, individual Democratic appointees vote in favor of the plan 81 percent of the time. It follows that an institution defending an affirmative action program has a one-in-three chance of success before an all-Republican panel—but more than a four-in-five chance before an all-Democratic panel! In a pattern that pervades many of the areas we explore, the rate of pro–affirmative action votes on all-Democratic panels is almost triple the corresponding rate of Republican votes on all-Republican panels.

## National Environmental Policy Act

NEPA, sometimes described as the Magna Carta of the environmental movement, is an important statute that essentially requires federal agencies to "consider" the environmental effects of all major federal actions significantly affecting the environment.[32] The "consideration" requirement is implemented through a mandate that agencies produce some kind of written assessment of environmental effects, sometimes through a formal environmental impact statement. NEPA has led to significant litigation, as parties challenge government action in order to stop or reorient projects of which they disapprove. Both pro-environment and pro-development petitioners bring suit seeking judicial enforcement of NEPA. The legal question is generally whether the agency

Figure 2-2. *Voting Patterns for Case Types with Both Party and Panel Effects*

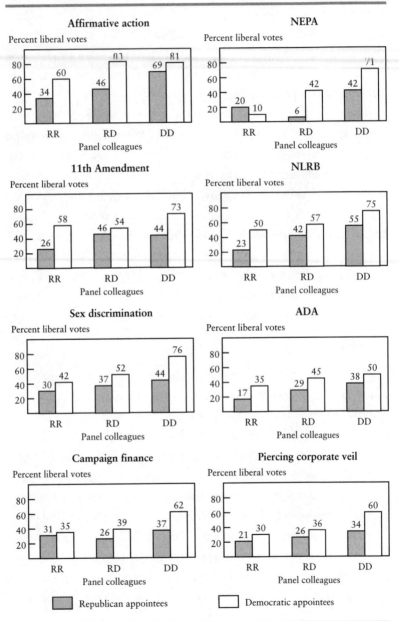

Figure 2-2. *Voting Patterns for Case Types with Both Party and Panel Effects* (continued)

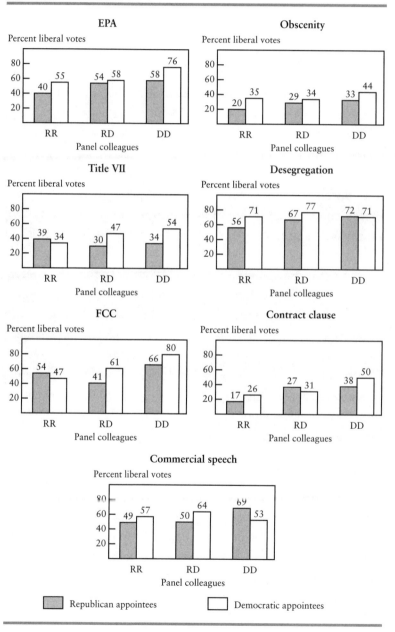

has met its obligation to consider the environmental impact of its actions; litigants often object that the environmental impact statement is inadequate.

A valuable data set documenting the success rates of NEPA plaintiffs has been compiled and analyzed by the Environmental Law Institute,[33] and we use that data set here. In cases from 2001 to 2004, Republican appointees vote on behalf of plaintiffs 20 percent of the time, whereas Democratic appointees do so 43 percent of the time. Hence there is significant evidence of ideological voting in this context.[34] There is also strong evidence of ideological dampening. A Democratic appointee sitting with two Republican appointees votes for a NEPA plaintiff just 10 percent of the time, while a Republican appointee sitting with two Democratic appointees votes for a NEPA plaintiff 42 percent of the time.

Democratic appointees also show evidence of ideological amplification. On all-Democratic panels, Democratic appointees vote for a NEPA plaintiff 71 percent of the time, compared with 42 percent on mixed Democratic majority panels. Interestingly, Republican appointees do not show ideological amplification. On all-Republican panels, Republican appointees vote for plaintiffs 20 percent of the time, but this number drops to 6 percent on mixed Republican majority panels. Because of the small numbers, however, this difference is not statistically significant.

*Eleventh Amendment*

One of the most contested areas in recent years has involved the immunity of states from damage awards under federal law. Conservative judges frequently argue that the Constitution's Eleventh Amendment creates a form of sovereign immunity, one that they are willing to read broadly; liberal judges frequently resist the idea of sovereign immunity on the part of the states. The stakes are often high, as litigants seek to obtain damages from state treasuries for violations of (for example) the Americans with Disabilities Act or the Age Discrimination in Employment Act.

A party difference can be found in judicial voting patterns. In cases since 1996 involving congressional abrogation of state sovereign immunity, Republican appointees vote to uphold abrogation 38 percent of the time, while Democratic appointees so vote 59 percent of the time. Hence the first hypothesis—ideological voting—is strongly supported.[35] The second hypothesis, involving ideological dampening, is confirmed as well. When sitting with two Democratic appointees, Republican appointees vote to uphold abrogation of state sovereign immunity 44 percent of the time. When sitting with two Republican appointees, Democratic appointees vote to uphold abrogation 58 percent of the time.

The third hypothesis, involving ideological amplification, is also confirmed. On all-Republican panels, Republican appointees vote to uphold abrogation only 26 percent of the time, while on all-Democratic panels, Democratic appointees vote to uphold abrogation 73 percent of the time—a remarkable 47 percent difference between the voting rates of Republican appointees on all-Republican panels and that of Democratic appointees on all-Democratic panels. The corresponding numbers on two-judge majority panels are 46 percent and 54 percent, respectively.

### National Labor Relations Board

The National Labor Relations Board is entrusted with implementation of the National Labor Relations Act, the most important statute governing labor unions. The decisions of the NLRB are often politically charged, and presidents attempt to reorient the agency in their preferred directions. Often the NLRB interprets provisions of the National Labor Relations Act, and the interpretations can be contentious. Under Republican presidents, for example, the NLRB is less likely to interpret ambiguous statutes in ways that labor unions like. Not infrequently, the NLRB's interpretations are challenged in court.

In cases involving these interpretations, we find powerful evidence of party effects: Democratic appointees vote in a stereotypically liberal direction 57 percent of the time, while Republican appointees do so 37 percent of the time.[36] We also find evidence of panel effects. There is ideological dampening: A Republican appointee sitting with two Democratic appointees issues a liberal vote 55 percent of the time, while a Democratic appointee sitting with two Republican appointees does so 50 percent of the time. There is also ideological amplification. A Republican appointee sitting with two other Republican appointees issues a liberal vote only 23 percent of the time, while a Democratic appointee sitting with two other Democratic appointees issues a liberal ruling a remarkable 75 percent of the time.

### Sex Discrimination

In sex discrimination cases from 1995 to 2004, Republican appointees voted in favor of plaintiffs 35 percent of the time, whereas Democratic appointees voted for plaintiffs 52 percent of the time. Hence we find strong evidence of ideological voting in this context.[37] We also find evidence of ideological dampening. When in the minority, Republican appointees vote in favor of sex discrimination plaintiffs 44 percent of the time, even higher than the 42 percent rate of Democratic appointees when they are in the minority.

The most striking number here is the remarkably high percentage of pro-plaintiff votes when three Democratic appointees are sitting together. Here, 76 percent of Democratic votes favor plaintiffs—far higher than the rates of 48 percent or less when Democratic appointees sit with one or more Republican appointees. On all-Republican panels, Republican appointees vote at a strongly anti-plaintiff rate, with only 30 percent favoring plaintiffs; this rate increases steadily with each Democrat on a panel.

## Disability

In disability discrimination cases collected for the period from 1998 to 2004,[38] the difference between Republican and Democratic appointees is substantial. Republican appointees vote for plaintiffs 27 percent of the time; Democratic appointees do so 43 percent of the time. Notably, those complaining of disability discrimination do not fare particularly well before either set of appointees, but the prospects are clearly better before Democrats.

Judges of both parties are generally influenced by the colleagues with whom they sit on a panel.[39] Sitting with one Republican and one Democrat, Republican appointees vote for plaintiffs at a rate of 29 percent, about the same as the aggregate figure. But when sitting with two Republican appointees, the rate drops to 17 percent, and when sitting with two Democratic appointees, it jumps to 38 percent. Democratic percentages move in the same directions, though with a slightly different pattern. The pro-plaintiff vote of 43 percent drops to 35 percent when a Democratic appointee sits with two Republican appointees (lower than the 38 rate for Republican appointees sitting with two Democratic appointees). It rises to 45 percent with one other Democrat and to 50 percent on all-Democratic panels. Here is another case of the standard pattern described in our three hypotheses.

## Sexual Harassment

Sexual harassment cases are a subset of sex discrimination cases; for that reason, they have not been included as a separate entry in our aggregate figures. But because the area is of considerable independent interest, we have conducted a separate analysis of sexual harassment cases. Republican appointees vote in favor of plaintiffs at a rate of 40 percent, whereas Democratic appointees vote for plaintiffs at a rate of 55 percent. Sitting with two Democratic appointees, Republican appointees are slightly more likely to vote for plaintiffs than Democratic appointees sitting with two Republican appointees by a margin of 49 percent to 46 percent. On all-Democratic panels, Democratic appointees vote for plaintiffs at a 72 percent rate, more than double the 35 percent rate of Republican appointees on all-Republican panels.[40]

### Campaign Finance

Campaign finance laws are often challenged on First Amendment grounds. Litigants contend that by restricting the ability to contribute to, or spend on, political campaigns, government is abridging the freedom of speech. We hypothesized that Republican appointees would be more sympathetic than Democratic appointees to this constitutional objection.

In cases since 1976, Republican appointees cast only 30 percent of their votes in favor of upholding campaign finance laws—substantially lower than the 44 percent rate for Democratic appointees. Because of the small sample size, the difference merely approaches statistical significance, and thus the first hypothesis—ideological voting—receives only tentative support.[41] With respect to the second hypothesis, involving ideological dampening, the results are suggestive as well. When sitting with two Democratic appointees, Republican appointees vote to uphold campaign finance laws 37 percent of the time. When sitting with two Republican appointees, Democratic appointees vote for such programs 35 percent of the time.

Now we turn to the third hypothesis, involving ideological amplification. On all-Republican panels, Republican appointees vote to uphold campaign finance regulations 31 percent of the time, while on all-Democratic panels, Democratic appointees vote to uphold such regulations 62 percent of the time. The corresponding numbers on two-judge majority panels are 26 percent and 39 percent, respectively. Thus, there is evidence of a substantial difference between the behavior of all-Democratic panels and Democratic majority panels—but Republican judges tend to vote similarly regardless of whether they are on unified panels or Republican majority panels.

### Piercing the Corporate Veil

Generally corporate officers are not personally liable for the misdeeds of their corporations. People can recover from the corporate treasury, not from the officers themselves. But in certain cases of egregious misconduct, there are exceptions to this rule, and when the corporation has no money, the only hope is to recover from the officers. When courts make exceptions, they are said to "pierce the corporate veil." We hypothesized, for obvious reasons, that Republican appointees would be more reluctant than Democratic appointees to allow the veil to be pierced.

Cases in which parties attempt to pierce the corporate veil follow our standard pattern, with all three hypotheses confirmed.[42] Republican appointees vote in favor of veil-piercing at a significantly lower rate than Democratic appointees: 25 percent as compared to 39 percent. But here, as elsewhere, Republicans sitting with two Democratic appointees, voting 34 percent in favor of veil-piercing, show more liberal voting patterns than Democrats sitting with two Republican appointees, voting in favor of veil-piercing only 30 percent of the time.

The most extreme figures in the data involve unified panels. Here, too, the pro-plaintiff voting percentage of Democratic appointees on all-Democratic panels is almost triple the corresponding number for Republican appointees on all-Republican panels: 60 percent as compared to 21 percent.

## Environmental Regulation

The Environmental Protection Agency issues regulations under a number of federal statutes designed to protect the environment. Those regulations are often challenged on legal grounds. Industry groups typically contend that the EPA has exceeded its legal authority through overzealous regulations. Public interest groups typically contend that the EPA should be more aggressive. Like the NLRB, the EPA must frequently interpret the statutes that it is asked to administer, and those interpretations are often challenged.

A large data set, modeled on that explored in an important and illuminating essay by Dean Richard Revesz,[43] comes from industry and public interest challenges to legal interpretations in EPA regulations.[44] From 1984 through 2004, Democratic appointees voted in a stereotypically liberal direction 61 percent of the time, whereas Republican appointees did so 51 percent of the time.[45]

There are also noteworthy panel effects.[46] Republican and Democratic appointees show ideological amplification and ideological dampening. On all-Republican panels, Republican appointees vote in a liberal direction just 40 percent of the time, but for members of two-Republican majorities this figure rises rapidly to 54 percent and finally to 58 percent for an isolated Republican appointee on a panel with two Democratic appointees. On all-Democratic panels, Democratic appointees vote in a liberal direction 76 percent of the time, but for members of two-Democratic majorities this figure falls to 58 percent and finally to 55 percent for a single minority Democrat.

## Obscenity

Are restrictions on sexually explicit materials unconstitutional? It might be expected that Republican appointees would be less sympathetic to constitutional challenges by those accused of unlawful obscenity; Republicans are less likely to believe that the first amendment protects the right to read obscene materials, and so the cases suggest. In cases since 1957, Republican appointees have ruled for obscenity defendants 27 percent of the time, while Democratic appointees have voted for such defendants 36 percent of the time.[47] Hence we find evidence of ideological voting. The second hypothesis, ideological dampening, is also supported on the Republican side. A Republican sitting with two Democratic appointees votes for a defendant 33 percent of the time. Interestingly, Democratic appointees do not reveal ideological dampening.

The third hypothesis, involving ideological amplification, is confirmed for both Republican and Democratic appointees. Republican appointees sitting on all-Republican panels vote for a constitutional challenge by a defendant only 20 percent of the time. A Democratic appointee sitting with two other Democratic appointees so votes 44 percent of the time.

## Title VII

The most important civil rights statute may well be Title VII of the Civil Rights Act of 1964, which forbids employment discrimination on the basis of race. Title VII actions often involve knotty issues of both law and fact, and those issues might well be expected to split Republican and Democratic appointees. In cases brought by African American plaintiffs, we find clear evidence of ideological voting: Democratic appointees vote for plaintiffs

43 percent of the time, whereas Republican appointees do so 34 percent of the time.[48]

Democratic appointees show both ideological dampening, with a 34 percent pro-plaintiff vote when sitting with two Republican appointees, and ideological amplification, with a 54 percent pro-plaintiff vote when sitting with two Democratic appointees. The pattern for Republican appointees is a puzzle. When sitting with two Republican appointees, Republican appointees actually vote for plaintiffs at a higher rate—39 percent—than when sitting with one or more Democratic appointees. When sitting with two Democratic appointees, Republican appointees vote for plaintiffs at a 34 percent rate, slightly higher than the 30 percent rate shown when sitting with one Democrat and one Republican. Overall, this pattern is similar to others with both party and panel effects, except for the apparently anomalous voting of all-Republican panels, for which we have no good explanation.

### Racial Segregation

*Brown* v. *Board of Education*, the case abolishing racial segregation in the United States, was decided in 1954.[49] Before *Brown*, a number of cases were brought in the lower courts, contending that "separate" was not "equal." Republican and Democratic appointees might be expected to differ in their responses to these challenges. After *Brown*, a large number of cases were brought, seeking compliance with the Court's mandate and also attempting to explore exactly what the Court meant to disallow. By the 1970s, new disputes broke out over "busing" remedies and a range of issues not squarely resolved by *Brown* itself. Here, too, party differences might well be expected.

In racial segregation cases brought between 1945 and 1985, we find evidence of ideological voting: Republican appointees vote against segregation 65 percent of the time, and Democratic appointees vote against segregation 74 percent of the time.[50] We also find evidence of ideological dampening on the Republican side: A Republican appointee sitting with two Democratic appointees votes against segregation 72 percent of the time. But Democratic appointees do not reveal much evidence of ideological dampening in this domain. A Democratic appointee sitting with two Republican appointees votes against segregation 71 percent of the time. Republican appointees also reveal ideological amplification. When sitting on unified Republican panels, a Republican appointee votes against segregation only 56 percent of the time. There is no evidence of ideological amplification among Democratic appointees. In chapter 5, we will return to the issue of segregation and will show some distinctive patterns over time.

*Federal Communications Commission*

Many of the most controversial regulatory decisions are made by the Federal Communications Commission, whose jurisdiction extends to a significant percentage of the national economy. Hence we investigated the question of whether our three hypotheses are valid in the context of judicial review of FCC interpretations of regulatory law. The area is parallel to those involving the NLRB and the EPA. Sometimes industry challenges the FCC's interpretation; sometimes the challenge is made by a public interest group. In this domain, it is sometimes difficult to "code" judicial decisions in ideological terms. For the sake of simplicity, we relied heavily on the identity of the challenger and hence generally treated a vote as liberal if it rejected an industry challenge and also if it favored a public industry challenge.

With this coding, we found evidence of ideological voting in FCC cases: In the period between 1984 and 2005, a Republican appointee votes in a stereotypically liberal direction 51 percent of the time, while a Democratic appointee does so 59 percent of the time.[51] There is also evidence of ideological dampening. When sitting with two Republicans, Democratic appointees vote in a liberal direction only 47 percent of the time—and when sitting with two Democratic appointees, Republican appointees vote in that direction 66 percent of the time. There is ideological amplification on the Democratic side: Democratic appointee sitting with two Democratic appointees issues a liberal ruling 80 percent of the time. Notably, however, there is no consistent evidence of ideological amplification on the Republican side. We are not sure how to explain this.

### Contracts Clause Violations

The Constitution's Contracts Clause forbids a state to enact any law impairing the obligation of contracts.[52] We examined Contracts Clause cases with the initial thought that Republican appointees would be more sympathetic than Democratic appointees to the claim that state governments had violated people's rights under the Contracts Clause. Our speculation to this effect was rooted in the fact that conservative academics have argued for stronger judicial protection of contractual rights through constitutional rulings.[53] But our speculation turned out to be wrong. There is mild evidence of ideological voting with respect to the Contracts Clause, but it runs in the opposite direction from what we predicted—apparently because those who make Contracts Clause objections, such as labor unions, are more sympathetic to Democratic than to Republican appointees.[54]

In cases from 1977 to 2004, Republican appointees vote on behalf of plaintiffs 25 percent of the time, whereas Democratic appointees do so 31 percent of the time. More striking in this context are the panel effects, which are large for both parties. On all-Democratic panels, Democratic appointees vote in favor of plaintiffs 50 percent of the time; on all-Republican panels, Republican appointees vote in favor of plaintiffs only 17 percent of the time.

Moreover, the dampening effects are large and in the predicted direction. Sitting with two Democratic appointees, Republican appointees vote in favor of plaintiffs in 38 percent of the cases, whereas a Democrat sitting with two Republican appointees does so just 26 percent of the time.

### First Amendment Challenges to Commercial Advertising Restrictions

Does the First Amendment protect commercial advertising? For a long time, the answer seemed to be no. The free speech principle is focused on democratic self-government, and for most of the nation's history, advertisers had nothing to gain from the First Amendment. Since 1976, however, the First Amendment has been understood to protect commercial advertising from legal restrictions.[55] The protection is not absolute. False and misleading advertising can be banned. In the last two decades, sharp disputes have arisen about the nature and the extent of the protection given to commercial advertisements.

It is generally thought that Republican appointees would be especially interested in protecting advertising. By common understanding, Democrats are less solicitous of the interests of business and more willing to allow government to attempt to protect consumers through regulation. The cases from 1978 through 2004 support this hypothesis: In the area of commercial advertising, we find evidence of party effects. Democratic appointees vote to uphold restrictions on commercial speech 59 percent of the time, while Republican appointees vote to uphold restrictions 53 percent of the time.[56]

There are also panel effects on the Republican side. Republican appointees show ideological dampening. On majority Democratic panels, Republican appointees vote to uphold restrictions on commercial advertising 69 percent of the time. Republican appointees also show ideological amplification. On all-Republican panels, Republican appointees vote to uphold restrictions 49 percent of the time. Democratic appointees show no panel effects in this domain.

## Courts, Not Judges

Thus far, we have focused on the votes of individual judges. For litigants and the law, of course, it is not the votes of individual judges, but the decisions of three-judge panels, that are of real interest. Let us now shift from individual votes to the outcomes of actual courts to see how our findings affect judicial decisions and the law.

In terms of the political affiliation of the appointing president, there are four possible combinations of judges on a three-judge panel: RRR, RRD, RDD, and DDD. Variations in panel composition can have two important effects, which should now be distinguished. The first, and simplest, involves the sheer number of people leaning in a certain direction. Suppose, for example, that Republican appointees are likely to vote in favor of particular programs only 40 percent of the time, whereas Democratic appointees are likely to vote in favor of such programs 70 percent of the time. As a simple statistical matter, and putting to one side the possibility that judges are influenced by one another, it follows that the likely majority outcome of a panel will be affected by its composition. Under the stated assumptions, a panel of all-Democratic appointees is far more likely (78 percent) to uphold the program than is a panel of two Democratic appointees and one Republican (66 percent), while an all-Republican panel is much less likely to do so (35 percent).[57]

This is an important and substantial difference. As noted, however, this statistical effect assumes that judicial votes are not influenced by judicial colleagues. Suppose, as we have found, that an individual judge's likely vote is in fact influenced by the composition of the panel. If so, then the mere majority force of predispositions, just described, will not tell the full story of the difference between all-Republican panels and all-Democratic panels. In fact, the statistical account will understate the difference, possibly substantially.

To illustrate with our own data, let us assume for the moment that the average percentages reported in the bottom row of table 2-1 do accurately represent individual voting tendencies for case types that show differences in panel decisions. Figure 2-3 compares the predicted percentages, based on 32 percent for Republican appointees and 48 percent for Democratic appointees and using the calculation above, to the observed averages from the same row of the table. The predicted panel effect (DDD% – RRR%) is 23 percent—but the observed effect is 35 percent. It is clear that, to explain these results, something must be at work other than majority voting with different ideological predictions.[58]

## Presidents and (Their?) Courts

With our method, it is possible to explore a range of additional questions, including judicial attitudes toward important decisions reached in different presidential administrations. A closely related essay, by Thomas Miles and one of the present authors, studies those attitudes in some detail.[59] The central goal of the study is to see whether political affiliation or political convictions play a role in judicial review of agency interpretations of law. Let us offer a brief overview by way of showing the generality of the findings we have been describing.

On the lower courts, the study involves all published court of appeals decisions between 1990 and the present, reviewing

Figure 2-3. *Predicted versus Actual Panel Decisions*[a]

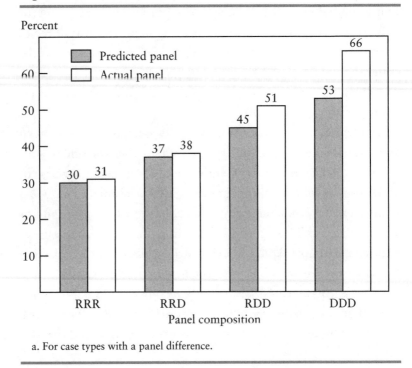

Percent

a. For case types with a panel difference.

interpretations of law by the EPA, the FCC, and the NLRB. These decisions are the same as those involved in the EPA, FCC, and NLRB data sets discussed in this chapter; the three are aggregated and analyzed to obtain a better sense of the relationship between judicial votes and particular administrations. Decisions are generally coded as "liberal" if the agency decision is upheld against industry attack; decisions are also generally coded as liberal if the agency decision is invalidated as a result of an attack by a public interest group. Here are the principal findings:

1. Republican appointees show significantly more conservative voting patterns than Democratic appointees. The former vote in

a liberal direction 48 percent of the time; the latter do so 59 percent of the time.

2. When Republican appointees sit only with Republican appointees, and when Democratic appointees sit only with Democratic appointees, the gap grows significantly—from 11 percent to 28 percent. Republican appointees show far more conservative voting patterns (43 percent liberal votes) when sitting only with other Republican appointees; the same is true for Democratic appointees on the liberal side (70 percent liberal votes). Hence ideological amplification is substantial.

3. Ideological dampening occurs as well. Sitting with two Republican appointees, Democratic appointees offer a liberal vote 52 percent of the time. Sitting with two Democratic appointees, Republican appointees offer a liberal vote 58 percent of the time. Here, then, is a context in which Democratic appointees, sitting with Republicans, turn out to be more conservative than Republican appointees, sitting with Democrats.

4. Republican appointees are more likely to uphold the interpretations of Republican administrations than those of Democratic administrations. Democratic appointees are more likely to uphold the interpretations of Democratic administrations than those of Republican administrations. This is a distinctive finding for the courts of appeals: There is a definite "tilt," on the part of federal judges, in the direction of administrations of the same political party as their appointing president.

The same study also explores the voting patterns of Supreme Court justices, to see whether party or ideology play a role in their voting behavior. Here, the data set involves all cases since 1994 in which the Supreme Court was asked to review an interpretation of law by the executive branch. Panel effects, of course, are difficult to assess for the Supreme Court, because nine justices are involved. But it is not difficult to put members of the Court into defined groups and to see how those groups compare with one another. Here are the main results:

1. Justices Antonin Scalia, Clarence Thomas, and William H. Rehnquist show significantly higher deference rates under the Bush administration than under the Clinton administration. Justices David Souter, John Paul Stevens, Stephen Breyer, and Ruth Bader Ginsburg show higher deference rates under the Clinton administration than under the Bush administration. Hence the Court's more conservative members are more likely to uphold the interpretations of the Bush administration, just as the Court's more liberal members are less likely to do so.

2. If decisions are coded in political terms, Justices Scalia, Thomas, and Rehnquist show the most conservative voting patterns in reviewing agency interpretations of law, while Justices Stevens, Souter, Breyer, and Ginsburg show the most liberal patterns.

3. When a justice is voting to reverse an agency's interpretation of law, what is the likelihood that the agency's decision will be liberal? For the Souter, Stevens, Breyer, and Ginsburg group, the likelihood is substantially under 50 percent; for the Scalia, Thomas, and Rehnquist group, the likelihood is substantially over 50 percent. Hence the liberal justices are more likely to reverse conservative decisions by the executive branch than liberal ones; the conservative justices show the opposite pattern.

These findings present many questions, and this is not the space to explore them in detail. The most straightforward point involves the courts of appeals: The simple pattern we have found in many contexts—of party effects and panels effects—cuts across judicial review of agency interpretations of law by the FCC, the EPA, and the NLRB, three of the nation's most important agencies. One consequence is that federal judges are especially likely to rule in favor of an administration that is run by a president of the same political party as the president who appointed them. And while the Supreme Court is not our focus here, it is more than interesting to see a degree of ideological voting on the nation's highest tribunal as well.

## Ideology, Dampening, and Amplification

The basic pattern, and some of our key findings, should now be clear. In numerous areas of the law, there is a substantial difference between the voting patterns of Republican and Democratic appointees. In this sense, ideological voting is emphatically present.

In many of the domains we have examined, both ideological dampening and ideological amplification are substantial. When Democratic appointees sit with two Republican appointees, they often show fairly conservative voting patterns. When Republican appointees sit with two Democratic appointees, they often show fairly liberal voting patterns. The most striking finding involves amplification, as both Democratic and Republican judges show more extreme tendencies when they are sitting with judges appointed by a president of the same party.

The upshot is straightforward. Because of party differences and panel effects, judicial decisions—both the results and the ultimate course of the law—are greatly affected by the composition of the panel. A litigant who draws three Democratic appointees will often have very different prospects than a litigant who draws three Republican appointees. As we shall see, ideological amplification is the most serious source of concern. But let us now turn to areas of law that defy the basic pattern that we have described thus far.

# Nonideological Voting and Entrenched Views

# 3

Our three hypotheses might be falsified in different ways. The most dramatic way of falsifying them would be to demonstrate that there is no difference between Republican appointees and Democratic appointees—that in relevant areas, the political party of the appointing president makes no difference. If this were so, then all three hypotheses would be proved wrong. Call this a finding of nonideological voting.

The most interesting, though more limited, way of falsifying them would be to show that party matters but that panel does not—that judges differ along predictable lines, but that their voting patterns are unaffected by the composition of the panel. If this were so, then our first hypothesis would be established, but not the second and third. Call this a finding of entrenched views. In this chapter, we explore areas in which both nonideological voting and entrenched views can be found.

## Where Party Doesn't Matter: Nonideological Voting

In five important areas, all of our hypotheses were rebutted (figure 3-1). The simple reason is that in these areas there is no significant difference between the votes of Republican appointees and those of Democratic appointees. Contrary to our own expectations, the political affiliation of the appointing president does not much matter in the contexts of criminal appeals, takings of private property, punitive damage awards, standing to sue, and Commerce Clause challenges to federal regulations. Let us explore these areas, and a few wrinkles, in sequence.

### Criminal Appeals

It might be anticipated that Democratic appointees would be especially sympathetic to criminal defendants and that Republican appointees would be relatively unsympathetic. At least this is a popular platitude about judicial behavior. Hence the three hypotheses might be anticipated to receive strong support. But all of them are rejected, at least in three courts of appeals from 1995 to the present.[1] We selected the courts of appeals for the D.C. Circuit and for the Third and Fourth Circuits on the theory that we would be highly likely to find ideological voting in criminal cases in those particular circuits. (We follow widespread, but informal, lore here, which suggests that ideological splits are especially severe on these circuits.) But we found no such effects. The overall rate of votes for defendants is between 31 percent and 37 percent, with only modest differences between Republican appointees and Democratic appointees and without significant panel effects. We conclude that Republican appointees and Democratic appointees do not much differ in this domain. One reason may well be that the two parties, and their judicial appointees, are not

Figure 3-1. *Voting Patterns for Case Types with Neither Party nor Panel Effects*

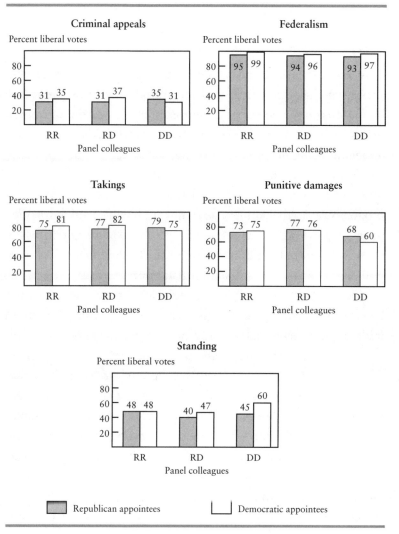

sharply divided on the rights of criminal defendants, as they likely were in earlier decades. We attempt to explain this finding in more detail in chapter 4.

### Federalism and the Commerce Clause

In the last two decades, there has been sharp disagreement about whether the federal judiciary should revive or strengthen limitations on the power of Congress. In particular, there has been intense debate on whether courts should restrict Congress's power under the Commerce Clause of the Constitution. Insisting that the power of the national government is limited, conservatives often favor such restrictions. Insisting that the Constitution gives broad power to the national government, liberals tend more often to reject these limitations. It might well be expected that Republican appointees would be far more likely than Democratic appointees to strike down federal legislation.

Since 1995, the overwhelming majority of federal judicial votes have been in favor of the constitutionality of programs challenged under the Commerce Clause. Indeed, Democratic appointees have voted to validate the challenged program 97 percent of the time! The numbers are not materially different for Republican appointees, for whom the overall validation rate is 94 percent. No panel effects are observed.[2] One qualification about our findings should be noted here: The difference between Republican and Democratic appointees is statistically significant. But this apparent difference is only of technical interest, since both groups of judges have voted to uphold nearly 100 percent of the time, and panels have voted to uphold at least 96 percent of the time regardless of the combination of judges (see table 2-1).

A possible reason for the agreement is that for many decades, the United States Supreme Court gave a clear signal that courts should be reluctant to invalidate congressional enactments under the Commerce Clause.[3] To be sure, the Court has provided important recent signs of willingness to invoke that clause against Congress.[4] But neither Republican nor Democratic appointees seem to believe that those signals should be taken very seriously. Perhaps things will change in this regard if the Court is more consistent about its message and as the lower courts internalize that message.

*Takings*

Across ideological lines, Americans believe in property rights. But in the culture as a whole, there seems to be a well-defined political division with respect to those rights. Conservatives are typically more interested in protecting property rights than liberals are. If an environmental regulation diminishes the value of property, Republicans are more likely than Democrats to object. This difference has been mirrored on the Supreme Court, as Justices Antonin Scalia and Clarence Thomas, both Republican appointees, are more likely to vote in favor of a property owner than are Justices Ruth Bader Ginsburg and Stephen Breyer, both Democratic appointees. But this difference does not map onto the behavior of judges on the federal courts of appeals.

The Takings Clause prohibits the confiscation, or "taking," of private property for public use without just compensation.[5] When plaintiffs challenge a governmental decision as violative of property rights, Democratic appointees and Republican appointees show no significant differences in voting.[6] Only 23 percent of Republican votes are in favor of such challenges. It might be expected that Democratic appointees would show a substantially lower percentage of votes in favor of property owners, but the rate for Democratic appointees is very close: 20 percent. No panel effects can be found. Note in this connection that our investigation did not include the United States Court of Federal Claims, where, according to informal lore, divisions across party lines are common.[7] It would be valuable to know whether a study of that court would uncover party and panel effects. But at least it can be said that on the ordinary courts of appeals, no difference can be found between Republican and Democratic appointees.

## Punitive Damages

A great deal of attention has recently been paid to punitive damage awards, by which juries punish wrongdoers by requiring them to pay noncompensatory (hence "punitive") damages to those whom they have harmed through defective products, pollution, or other wrongdoing.[8] Sometimes these damage awards are substantial, coming in the millions or even billions of dollars. Many Republican politicians, including President George W. Bush, have expressed serious concerns about punitive awards. Democratic politicians have typically been more sympathetic to them, apparently seeing jury awards as an important way of deterring and punishing misconduct. (It may be that the behavior of Democratic politicians is attributable to the influence of American trial lawyers, who contribute a great deal to campaigns.)

In this light, it might well be thought that Democratic appointees would be more likely than Republican appointees to uphold punitive damage awards. And indeed, there are a range of legal limits, including constitutional limits, on excessive or arbitrary punitive awards. But when parties challenge such awards as legally excessive, Republican appointees and Democratic appointees show no differences in their voting patterns. From 1987 to 2004, Republican appointees vote to uphold punitive damage awards 74 percent of the time, and Democratic appointees vote to uphold such awards 73 percent of the time.[9] There are no panel effects. On federal courts of appeals, Republican appointees are not more hostile to punitive damage awards than are Democratic appointees.

## Standing

The law of "standing" is technical but exceedingly important; it determines parties' access to federal court. In the 1960s and 1970s, federal courts altered the law so as to allow an increasing number of individuals and groups to raise legal challenges.[10] In cases involving the environment and telecommunications, for example, public-interest groups were frequently permitted to complain that the government had failed to do enough to implement regulatory programs. If listeners wanted to complain about the FCC's failure to promote public-interest programming on the radio, or if those living next to a river objected to the EPA's failure to enforce an antipollution law, the courts were generally available. The last fifteen years have seen a modest backlash.[11] On the Supreme Court, conservative judges seem more likely to rule that parties lack standing to invoke the federal judiciary; and conservative judges are more likely to be appointed by Republican presidents.

Among the courts of appeals, the most important in this domain is the United States Court of Appeals for the District of Columbia Circuit, which resolves a large number of disputes about who has standing to sue the federal government. It would be expected that Democratic appointees to that court would be far more likely than Republican appointees to allow people to bring suit. But in standing cases in the D.C. Circuit between 1990 and 2004, we find no statistically significant evidence of ideological voting: Republican appointees vote to find standing 44 percent of the time, and Democratic appointees vote to find standing 49 percent of the time.[12] Republican appointees reveal no panel effects in this domain. A Republican appointee is actually more likely to vote to find standing (a 48 percent liberal voting rate) when sitting with two other Republicans than when sitting on mixed (40 percent rate) or minority Republican panels (45 percent rate).

For Democratic appointees, there is a hint of a panel effect, but it is too small (and nonsignificant) to be taken very seriously. A Democratic appointee sitting with two Democratic appointees votes in favor of standing 60 percent of the time; a Democratic appointee sitting with two Republican appointees so votes 48 percent of the time. A qualification: The sample size is not large, and the party difference does approach statistical significance. It would have been reasonable, however, to expect a clear difference along party lines, and the absence of such a difference is noteworthy.

## Entrenched Views:
## The Cases of Abortion and Capital Punishment
*(with a speculative note on gay and lesbian rights)*

In ordinary life, people's views are often influenced by others. As we shall later see in some detail, conformity is an important aspect of the human condition. At first glance, ideological dampening appears to be a conformity effect: Republican appointees look rather like Democratic appointees when they sit only with Democratic appointees, and Democratic appointees, in the presence of Republican appointees, turn out to look like Republican appointees. In addition, like-minded people have a tendency to go to extremes; ideological amplification may well reflect a process of that kind. But some of the time, people's views are entrenched and therefore impervious to what others think. We might expect that when positions are intensely held, they are less likely to shift in the presence of competing views.

Figure 3-2. *Voting Patterns for Case Types with Only a Party Effect*

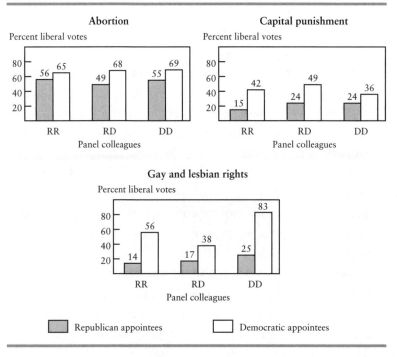

It is possible to imagine areas of the law that show a pattern of entrenchment and hence imperviousness to others. In such areas, ideological voting is definitely present, in the sense that judges are expected to vote in a way that reflects the political affiliation of the appointing president; but panel effects are minimal or nonexistent. It might be expected that the pattern of entrenched views would be found in multiple areas, but it occurred in only two areas that we investigated: abortion and capital punishment (see figure 3-2).

In abortion cases since 1971, Democratic appointees have cast pro-choice votes 67 percent of the time, compared to 51 percent for Republican appointees. This is substantial evidence of ideological voting.[13] (Note that the high rate of pro-choice votes, for Republican appointees, need not be attributed to pro-choice political convictions on the part of such appointees. Often the law is clear, and judges must follow it whatever their convictions; note as well the 33 percent voting rate *against* abortion rights by Democratic appointees.) But panel effects are absent. Sitting with two Democratic appointees, Republican appointees vote in favor of abortion rights 55 percent of the time—a figure that is not appreciably different from the 51 percent rate when sitting with one or more Republican appointees or from the 56 percent pro-choice rate in all-Republican panels. Similarly, sitting with two Republican appointees, Democratic appointees vote in favor of abortion rights 65 percent of the time—not much less than the 68 percent and 69 percent rates when sitting with one or two other Democratic appointees, respectively.

The absence of ideological amplification is even more striking. A Republican vote on an all-Republican panel is slightly more likely to be liberal than a Republican vote on a panel of two Republican appointees and one Democrat. But the difference is not statistically significant, and hence Republican votes are essentially impervious to panel effects. A Democratic vote on an all-Democratic panel is approximately the same as a Democratic vote on a panel of two Democratic appointees and one Republican.

Capital punishment shows a similar pattern: a large party difference but no significant panel effects.[14] Republican appointees vote for defendants 15 percent of the time on all-Republican panels, 24 percent of the time on majority Republican panels, and 24 percent of the time on majority Democratic panels. Democratic appointees vote for defendants 36 percent of the time on all-Democratic panels, 49 percent of the time on majority Democratic panels, and 42 percent of the time on majority Republican panels. Here, then, is another area in which views are entrenched.

A third area, possibly analogous to those just mentioned, involves gay and lesbian rights. In the relatively small number of cases ($n = 22$) since 1980, Democratic appointees have voted in favor of plaintiffs 57 percent of the time, while Republican appointees have done so only 16 percent of the time.[15] Hence we find extremely strong evidence of ideological voting—the strongest evidence, in terms of raw percentages, of all of our case categories. Indeed, the party difference is so marked that it is statistically significant even with this small sample of cases. Perhaps this is unsurprising, because the issue of gay and lesbian rights causes intense political conflict in general.

The shape of the graph would appear to suggest the presence of ideological dampening and amplification. But because of the small sample, these apparent differences are not statistically significant. Until a larger body of decisions is available, the presence or absence of a panel effect must remain an open question.

What explains these various findings? What explains ideological dampening and ideological amplification? We now turn to these questions.

# Explaining the Data

# 4

## Conformity, Group Polarization, and the Rule of Law

W hat accounts for these patterns? Why are our three hypotheses sometimes confirmed and sometimes rejected? For purposes of analyzing our findings, we should distinguish among three categories of cases: nonideological voting; entrenched views; and the ordinary pattern of cases, in which all three hypotheses are confirmed.

### Nonideological Voting: No Party Effects, No Panel Effects

Consider first the contexts in which all three of our hypotheses are rejected. In those contexts, Republican and Democratic appointees do not much disagree, and hence the political party of the appointing president will not affect outcomes. In many areas, the political affiliation of the appointing president is undoubtedly irrelevant to judicial votes. For example, we would not expect to see significant party effects in cases that present routine issues of state law; political differences simply do not matter there. Where Republicans and Democrats do not disagree, there should be no difference between Republican and Democratic appointees to the federal bench. But our investigation finds that party is irrelevant in several areas where such effects might be anticipated, and indeed in which we ourselves anticipated them. By informal lore, Republican appointees and Democratic appointees do disagree in criminal appeals and in cases involving takings, punitive damages, standing to sue, and federalism. But informal lore turns out to be wrong. There are two possible explanations. The first involves *binding law*; the second involves *bipartisan consensus* among judges.

In some areas, the law (as established by Congress, the Supreme Court, or by previous appellate decisions) is clear and binding, and hence ideological disagreements cannot materialize. It is plausible to think that in all five areas, governing law dampens any differences between Republican and Democratic appointees. At the court of appeals level, precedents or congressional enactments might well be clear enough to overcome the potential effects of party. To be sure, the word "enough" is crucial here. If the law is entirely clear, people will not litigate, and if they lose, an appeal will be unlikely. By definition, the cases that reach the courts of appeals have at least some degree of uncertainty. But it remains possible that in those courts, the law often has two characteristics: enough play to justify an appeal but also enough clarity to reduce or eliminate ideological disagreements. In some areas, those disagreements will manifest themselves mostly or only in the "frontiers" cases—the highly unusual situations that find their way to the Supreme Court itself. It follows that the absence of party effects, within the courts of appeals, is plausibly a product of the discipline that the law imposes.

This hypothesis finds some support in the Commerce Clause area, where Democratic and Republican appointees almost always agree, and the small difference between them seems to come only in these "frontiers" cases. For criminal appeals, there is a further point. Unlike in the civil context, criminal defendants will appeal even when the law is fairly clearly against them, because (with rare exceptions) they are not paying for the appeal. Because their liberty is on the line, and because economic incentives do not discipline appeals, convicted criminals will often seek appellate review even if it is most unlikely that they will prevail. As a result, most criminal appeals lack merit under the existing doctrine.[1]

We are not sure whether the law is clear enough to explain the high degree of consensus in cases involving punitive damages, standing to sue, and takings of private property. But even when the doctrine does allow courts room to maneuver, appointees of different parties may not much disagree about the appropriate principles in certain areas. Here, then, is our second explanation for the absence of party effects: bipartisan consensus. Notwithstanding political differences within the nation at large, the disagreements within the judiciary might be narrow or even nonexistent. Splits between Republicans and Democrats might not be mirrored by splits between Republican and Democratic appointees to the federal bench. Other empirical work suggests that in criminal cases, President Clinton's appointees do not differ from Republican appointees.[2] Within the federal courts of appeals, a near consensus across partisan lines appears to exist in the area of criminal law. Perhaps the same is true in the contexts of takings, standing to sue, federalism, and punitive damages.

Our data do not allow us to decide between the "binding precedent" and "bipartisan consensus" accounts. But they do establish the important point that in some domains where Democratic appointees and Republican appointees might be expected to differ, there is essential agreement. In these contexts, we find a tribute to conventional aspirations for the rule of law.[3] Perhaps the law is effectively controlling; perhaps judges do not differ in their predispositions. In either case, similarly situated litigants will be treated similarly.

## Party Effects without Panel Effects

What about the contexts of abortion and capital punishment? (We bracket gay and lesbian rights, on the ground that the sample size is too small.) Here we find that party affiliation is what matters, and hence that judges will be affected by their convictions regardless of the composition of the panel. In these cases, the antecedent convictions of federal judges must be extremely strong—strong enough to undo the panel influences that occur in other types of cases. It does seem clear that judges have strong beliefs about abortion and capital punishment, issues about which people's beliefs are often fiercely held. In cases of this kind, it is natural to assume that votes will be relatively impervious to panel effects.[4] In the next chapter, we shall discover some complexities in the context of abortion, but it remains true that in that area, judges are relatively impervious to the positions of their colleagues.

The disaggregated data show that for some judges, other areas have similar characteristics. On the D.C. Circuit, Democratic appointees respond to challenges to environmental regulations in the same way that judges as a whole respond to abortion and capital punishment cases: They are unaffected by the different influences that come from different panel compositions. We find neither ideological dampening nor ideological amplification. For Democratic appointees, party matters, but panel does not. Interestingly, Republican appointees on the D.C. Circuit show strong panel influences. In general, Sixth Circuit judges show the same pattern as Democrats on the D.C. Circuit in cases challenging environmental regulations; whatever their party, judges on the Sixth Circuit are not much affected by their colleagues.

How can we explain such patterns? One possibility is that the relevant judges have strong convictions across a range of cases—convictions that are sufficient to make panel irrelevant. Perhaps this is true for Democratic appointees assessing environmental cases on the D.C. Circuit. Another possibility is that in some times and places, judges of the opposing party are particularly unconvincing. On the Sixth Circuit, there might be a high degree of separation (personal or ideological) between Republican and Democratic appointees, so that dampening occurs little if at all. To understand this possibility, it is necessary to explore the reasons for panel effects.

## Why Panel Effects?

In our data, the usual pattern involves not simply party effects but also panel effects. Indeed, the latter are as large as the former and sometimes larger. What is the explanation? We suggest that three factors are probably at work: conformity, group polarization, and whistleblowing. These factors have considerable power in explaining the patterns that we observe. They also provide a clue to human behavior in many contexts.

### Conformity, Entrenched Views, and the Collegial Concurrence

In the particular context of judicial review of environmental regulations, a careful analysis by Dean Richard Revesz finds that "while individual ideology and panel composition both have important effects on a judge's vote, the ideology of one's colleagues is a better predictor of one's vote than one's own ideology."[5] In the same vein, we have found a number of areas in which the political party of the president who appointed the other judges on the panel is often a good predictor of a judge's vote. But what makes "the ideology of one's colleagues" so influential? Let us begin by focusing on ideological dampening—the possibility that a judge's ideological tendencies will be moderated when sitting with two judges appointed by a president of another political party.

The simplest explanation is that much of the time, judges are willing to offer a *collegial concurrence*, which we define as a concurrence based on deference to one's colleagues. Apparently the collegial concurrence is a pervasive feature of behavior on the federal bench. Because of the collegial concurrence, Republican appointees show fairly liberal voting patterns when sitting with two Democratic appointees, and Democratic appointees show fairly conservative voting patterns when sitting with two Republican appointees. But why does the collegial concurrence occur? Why are isolated judges so likely to be influenced by their colleagues?

*1. Behind the collegial concurrence.* We suggest that two factors contribute to the collegial concurrence. First, the votes of one's colleagues carry pertinent information about what is right. If two colleagues believe that an affirmative action program is unconstitutional, then there is reason to think that the program is indeed unconstitutional. If two colleagues think that disability discrimination has occurred, in violation of the law, there is reason to conclude that such discrimination has indeed occurred. A single judge, confronted with those views, will have reason to agree with them. Second, dissenting opinions on a three-judge panel are likely to be both futile and highly burdensome to produce—a discouraging combination. Most of the time, such dissents will not persuade either of the majority's judges to switch his vote. To be sure, such a dissent might, in extreme cases, attract the attention of the Supreme Court or lead to a rehearing by the full circuit (rehearing "en banc"); and when judges dissent, it is sometimes in the hope that such an outcome will occur. Supreme Court review is rare, however, and courts of appeals do not often rehear cases en banc.

In any case, it can be quite time-consuming to write a dissent. If the ultimate decision is not going to be affected, why do the extra work? Confronted with the contrary view of two colleagues, a reasonable judge might well conclude that his own position might well be wrong, and in any event it is not worthwhile to press the disagreement in public. A collegial concurrence might well result from a simple calculus: The majority view may be right, and in any case, a dissenting opinion will not do any good even if the majority is wrong.

There are further points. Our data capture votes rather than opinions. For the actual development of the law, the opinion matters a great deal. The majority might strike down an affirmative action program or a campaign finance regulation, but it might do so with an opinion that leaves open the possibility that other affirmative action programs, or other campaign finance regulations, will be upheld in the future. Perhaps Democratic appointees show a conservative voting pattern when sitting with two Republicans; but perhaps they are able to affect the court's opinion by moving it in the direction of greater moderation. To the extent that this is so, the effect of the isolated judge is significantly understated by our data; that effect can be measured only by examining opinions for their moderation or extremism (a possibility to which we shall return). And in fact we suspect that a sole Republican appointee, or a sole Democratic appointee, often does have a greater impact than is found by an examination of votes alone. If an isolated judge can ensure a moderated opinion, his effect might well be substantial. In short, the isolated judge might accept the outcome, but only after ensuring that it does not damage legal principles to which the judge subscribes. A judge might offer a collegial concurrence because that very judge has affected the opinion in which he has concurred.

In any case, dissenting opinions might also cause a degree of tension among judges—a particular problem in light of the fact that the same judges often work together for many years. According to informal lore, a kind of implicit bargain is struck within many courts of appeals, in the form of, "I won't dissent from your opinions if you won't dissent from mine, at least not unless the disagreement is very great." Sometimes judges go along with results with which they do not really agree, expecting and receiving a degree of reciprocity; and reciprocity therefore contributes to ideological dampening on all sides. In these circumstances, it should be no surprise that Republican appointees show fairly liberal voting patterns when sitting with two Democratic appointees, or that Democratic appointees show fairly conservative voting patterns when sitting with two Republican appointees.

All of these points help to account for the great power of "the ideology of one's colleagues" in producing judicial votes. In particular, these points help to account for ideological dampening. It would be interesting in this regard to learn whether judges are less likely to dissent when they are newly appointed or when they have been on the bench for an extended period. We could speculate either way here. Perhaps judges learn that reciprocity is extremely important and hence are less likely to dissent as time passes; perhaps new judges are especially collegial in the relevant sense and therefore show a special degree of reciprocity in their early years. It would also be interesting to learn whether judges are less likely to dissent when their chambers are physically close to other chambers and hence when judges see each other on a regular basis. Note in this regard that in the Sixth Circuit, where tensions across party lines are often said to run high, there has been an evident breakdown of reciprocity, simply because ideological dampening does not occur.

2. *Conformity*. We can better understand these points if we notice the clear connection between the collegial concurrence and the behavior of ordinary people in experimental settings when faced with the opinion of unanimous others. A great deal of social science research has demonstrated that if people are confronted with a unanimously held view, they tend to yield.[6] This finding has been made in the context of both political and legal issues.[7] In fact, experiments find huge conformity effects for many judgments about morality and politics,[8] including issues involving civil liberties, ethics, and crime and punishment.

Consider the following statement: "Free speech being a privilege rather than a right, it is proper for a society to suspend free speech when it feels threatened." Asked to evaluate this question individually, only 19 percent of the control group agreed. But confronted with the unanimous agreement of four others, 58 percent of people agreed! In a similar finding, subjects were asked: "Which one of the following do you feel is the most important problem facing our country today?" Five alternatives were offered: economic recession, educational facilities, subversive activities, mental health, and crime and corruption. Asked privately, 12 percent chose subversive activities. But when exposed to a spurious group consensus unanimously selecting that option, 48 percent of people made the same choice. Questioned privately, not one military officer agreed with the following statement: "I doubt whether I would make a good leader." But confronted with a unanimous group apparently accepting that statement, 37 percent of officers agreed.[9]

Indeed, conformity can influence people's judgment on simple issues of fact.[10] In some famous experiments, Solomon Asch explored whether people would be willing to overlook the apparently unambiguous evidence of their own senses.[11] In these experiments, the subject was placed into a group of seven to nine people who seemed to be other subjects in the experiment but who were actually Asch's confederates. The ridiculously simple task was to "match" a particular line, shown on a large white card, to the one of three "comparison lines" that was identical to it in length. The two non-matching lines were substantially different, with the differential varying from an inch and three-quarters to three-quarters of an inch.

In the first two rounds of the Asch experiments, everyone agrees about the right answer. "The discriminations are simple; each individual monotonously calls out the same judgment."[12] But "suddenly this harmony is disturbed at the third round."[13] All other group members make what is obviously, to the subject and to any reasonable person, a big error, matching the line at issue to one that is conspicuously longer or shorter. In these circumstances, the subject has a choice: He can maintain his independent judgment or instead accept the view of the unanimous majority. Remarkably, most people end up yielding to the group at least once in a series of trials. When asked to decide on their own, without seeing judgments from others, people erred less than 1 percent of the time. But in rounds in which group pressure supported the incorrect answer, people erred 36.8 percent of the time.[14] Indeed, in a series of twelve questions, no fewer than 70 percent of people went along with the group, and defied the evidence of their own senses, at least once.[15]

People's yielding—a form of collegial concurrence—occurs for two different reasons. The first involves the information offered by the unanimous view of others. If everyone else subscribes to a certain position, perhaps they are right. How could such shared views be wrong? The second reason involves reputational pressures. People do not want to go out on a limb for fear that others will disapprove of them.

Our evidence suggests that judges are vulnerable to similar influences. As we have suggested, the shared view of the other two judges on the panel contains information about what is right, just as in the conformity experiments. And while judges sitting on three-member panels might not be concerned with their reputations in the same way as subjects in psychology experiments, social dynamics, discouraging frequent statements of public disagreement, operate in an analogous way. It is not especially comfortable for a judge to disagree with the view of two colleagues, at least not on a routine basis. Especially because federal judges frequently sit together on panels, the informal norm, captured in a general reluctance to dissent, serves the interest of collegiality.

3. *Entrenchment.* An understanding of collegial concurrences helps to explain the failure of the second and third hypotheses in the contexts of abortion and capital punishment. In those contexts, people's judgments tend to be firmly held. The firmness of those judgments is apparently sufficient to outweigh whatever pressures are imposed by the contrary judgments of panel members. Note here that when judgments are firm, it is only in particular subsets of these cases. Even in areas in which views are intensely held, it is not as if Democratic appointees vote in a liberal direction 100 percent of the time and Republican appointees 0 percent of the time; for both abortion and capital punishment, the overlap in views is significant. Apparently there are two sets of

cases in both domains: those in which everyone agrees on the outcome that the law dictates, and those in which the law leaves uncertainty that serves to split judges along identifiably partisan lines. In the second set of cases, the percentages are probably closer to 100 percent for Democratic appointees and 0 percent for Republican appointees. The overall percentage mixes the two sets of cases.

What we are emphasizing here is the fact that judges appear to be impervious to panel effects in the second set of cases. If judges have extremely clear views about a legal question involving abortion, they might well be unmoved by the "information" provided by the opinions of other judges on the panel. And if their views on the abortion issue are intensely held, they might well be willing to take the trouble to produce a dissenting opinion, even if it is burdensome to do so and not much appreciated by the court's majority.

Judges, no less than ordinary people, are more likely to resist conformity pressures if their own beliefs are firmly held. There is a related point. For certain highly charged issues, a given judge's convictions may be well known to be firmly held by the other judges on that panel, and thus those judges are less likely to perceive a dissent as a failure of collegiality.

4. *Dampening, leveling, and moderation.* In fact, an understanding of the relevant processes helps to explain and refine the dampening and leveling effects that we have emphasized. Suppose that a Democratic appointee is sitting with two Republican appointees; suppose, too, that everyone on the panel knows that the Democratic appointee might reject an extreme ruling. For the reasons that we have sketched, a dissent or a separate opinion may be unlikely. But the mere possibility of a dissent might lead the two Republicans to moderate their ruling so as to ensure unanimity. The collegial concurrence need not signify that the iso-

lated Democrat, or the isolated Republican, is simply going along with her peers. The very presence of a potential dissenter can lead to a mutually agreeable opinion; both sides might have done some yielding. For this reason, as noted, our finding of ideological dampening may well understate the influence of the isolated Democrat or the isolated Republican, who may be moving the law in general if not the result in particular.

We have emphasized that our data, focused on outcomes, do not enable us to test this hypothesis rigorously. But the sharp difference between divided and unified panels, in terms of expected votes, is at least suggestive of the possibly important effect of the isolated Democrat or Republican. It is to that effect that we now turn.

## Group Polarization

Why do all-Republican panels and all-Democratic panels behave so distinctively? Why are they different from majority Republican panels and majority Democratic panels? A clue comes from one of the most striking findings in modern social science: *Deliberating groups of like-minded people tend to go to extremes.*[16] More particularly, deliberating groups typically end up adopting a more extreme view in the same direction as their predeliberation median. Consider a few examples outside of the context of judicial behavior:

—A group of moderately profeminist women becomes more strongly profeminist after discussion.[17]

—After discussion, citizens of France become more critical of the United States and its intentions with respect to economic aid.[18]

—After discussion, whites predisposed to show racial prejudice offer more negative responses to the question of whether white racism is responsible for conditions faced by African-Americans in American cities.[19]

—After discussion, whites predisposed not to show racial prejudice offer more positive responses to the same question.[20]

—After discussion, juries inclined to award punitive damages typically produce awards that are significantly higher than the awards specified, before discussion, by the median member.[21]

—After discussion, liberals show more liberal positions on affirmative action, civil unions, and American participation in a global effort to control global warming; after discussion, conservatives show more conservative positions on the same issues.[22]

There is good reason to believe that ideological amplification, as we have defined it, is a reflection of group polarization. To be sure, we do not have a "pure" test of group polarization; there is no record of judges' votes before deliberation begins. Recall that we measure amplification by comparing judicial votes on unified panels to judicial votes on divided panels. But it is reasonable to think that group polarization is indeed at work if Republican and Democratic appointees both show stronger ideological tendencies when sitting only with judges appointed by a president of the same political party.

Indeed, an understanding of group polarization strongly suggests that, in an important sense, our findings about ideological amplification are actually understated (just as our findings about ideological dampening may well be overstated). Recall that we have focused on votes—on who wins and who loses—without focusing on opinions, which can be written narrowly or broadly. Investigation of the substance of the opinions would obviously be burdensome and involve considerable discretion on the part of the investigator. But it is plausible to speculate that a unified panel is far less likely to be moderate than a divided one is—and hence that an investigation that looks only at likely votes greatly understates the extremism of all-Republican and all-Democratic panels.

When a panel consists only of Republican appointees, an opinion striking down an affirmative action program might not merely strike down an affirmative action program; it might also set up a broad rule, opposing affirmative action programs in most or all circumstances. When a panel consists only of Democratic appointees, an opinion upholding a campaign finance regulation might not merely uphold a particular regulation; it might also suggest that campaign finance regulations are generally acceptable. Much room remains for further analysis here. Our own examination of the cases, which is anecdotal rather than formal and systematic, does indeed suggest that unified panels often write relatively extreme opinions. We are willing to speculate that there is an empirical regularity here.

There have been three main explanations for group polarization, all of which have been extensively investigated.[23]

1. *Persuasive arguments.* The first explanation, emphasizing the role of persuasive arguments, is based on a common-sense intuition: any individual's position on an issue is partly a function of which arguments presented within the group are convincing. People's judgments move in the direction of the most persuasive position defended by the group, taken as a collectivity. Suppose that a group's members are already inclined to vote in support of a certain conclusion—say, that global warming is a serious problem. Within that group, there will be a disproportionate number of arguments supporting the conclusion that global warming is a serious problem. If people are listening to one another, the result of discussion will be to move people further in the direction of their initial belief that global warming is a serious problem. The key is the existence of a limited argument pool, one that is skewed in a particular way.

In the context of appellate judging, we think that this is probably the best explanation of our finding of the relative extremism of all-Democratic and all-Republican tribunals. If two members of the panel conclude that an affirmative action program is unconstitutional, or that a disability claim has not been established, the third judge has good reason to accept that conclusion. This process is reinforced by the natural human tendency toward *confirmation bias*, by which people find most compelling those arguments that confirm their antecedent inclinations.[24] Hence it should be no surprise that like-minded judges show ideological amplification. Things are very different if our third judge is confronted with a split between her two colleagues, offering reasons in both directions.

2. *Social comparison.* The second explanation, involving social comparison, begins with the claim that people want other group members to perceive them favorably—and they also want to perceive themselves favorably. Once they hear what others believe, they sometimes adjust their positions in the direction of the dominant view. The result is to press the group's position toward one or another extreme and also to induce shifts in individual members.[25] People may wish, for example, not to seem too enthusiastic about, or too restrained in their enthusiasm for, affirmative action, gun control, protection against global warming, or an increase in national defense; hence their views may shift when they see what other group members think. One result of social comparison will be group polarization.

Does social comparison play a role in the voting behavior of federal judges? Any answer would be highly speculative. But it is at least possible that interactions among judges, extending over time, make it more likely that in controversial areas of law, Democratic appointees will be inclined to attend to the inclinations of other Democratic appointees and that Republican appointees will do the same with other Republican appointees. If, for example, a Democratic appointee is sitting with two other

Democratic appointees, both of whom want to rule in favor of someone complaining of disability discrimination, there might well be at least some pressure to accept the dominant opinion. Of course, this pressure can be, and sometimes is, resisted. But across a large number of cases, there might be some movement in the direction of ideological amplification.

3. *The role of corroboration.* The third explanation begins by noting that people with extreme views tend to have more confidence that they are right, and that as people gain confidence they become more extreme in their beliefs.[26] The basic idea is simple: Those who lack confidence, and who are unsure what they think, tend to moderate their views. It is for this reason that cautious people, not knowing what to do, are likely to choose the midpoint between relevant extremes.[27] If other people seem to share your view, however, you are likely to become more confident that you are correct—and hence to move in a more extreme direction. In a wide variety of experimental contexts, people's opinions have been shown to become more extreme simply because their view has been corroborated, and because they have become more confident after learning of the shared views of others.[28] For example, those who tend to believe that global warming is a serious problem are likely to become more intensely committed to that belief after being confirmed in that belief by others.

Does this explanation account for ideological amplification on federal courts of appeals? It is certainly possible. Perhaps judges are more tentative when they are sitting with people of diverse views, in general or on particular issues. Perhaps judicial inclinations become hardened as a result of corroboration, thus producing the distinctive voting patterns of judges on unified panels. Perhaps judicial opinions become more extreme when judges are sitting with like-minded others. Because corroboration of opinion leads to greater confidence, and hence to extremity, it is not surprising that deliberation by a panel of three like-minded judges would lead to ideological amplification.

Suppose, for example, that three judges are tentatively inclined to strike down an affirmative action program. For each judge, the initial inclination to that effect will be strengthened by the corroboration by two others. Hence the likelihood of a vote to invalidate will be increased—and the resulting opinion is likely to be more extreme as well. For this reason, we might well predict an increased likelihood of stereotypically liberal outcomes when Democratic appointees are sitting on panels consisting solely of Democratic appointees. The best test of the corroboration hypothesis would involve judicial opinions, not merely votes. But on the basis of the evidence here, involving votes rather than opinions, it is likely that corroboration is playing a real role.

Whatever the precise explanation, ideological amplification on all-Republican and all-Democratic panels reflects group polarization. When a court consists of a panel of judges appointed by presidents of the same political party, the median view before deliberation begins will often be significantly different from what it would be in a panel with a mix of Democratic and Republican appointees. The "argument pool" will likely be very different as well. For example, a panel of three Republican appointees, tentatively inclined to invalidate the action of the Environmental Protection Agency, will offer a range of arguments in support of invalidation and relatively fewer in the other direction—and this may be so even if the law, properly interpreted, favors validation. But if the panel contains a judge who is inclined to uphold the EPA, the arguments that favor validation are far more likely to emerge and to be pressed. Indeed, the very fact that the judge is a Democratic appointee increases the likelihood that such counterarguments will emerge, since that judge might not think of himself as being entirely part of the same "group" as the other panel members. Group polarization is more likely, and larger, when people think of themselves as belonging to a single "group," defined in political or other terms.[29]

At this point, a skeptic might note that lawyers make adversarial presentations before judges. Such a skeptic might insist that the size of the "argument pool" is determined by those presentations, not only—and not even mostly—by what members of the panel are inclined to say and do. And there can be no question that the inclinations of judges are shaped, much of the time, by the contributions of advocates. But this point cannot explain our findings here: Adversarial presentations are made before all possible panel compositions, and hence they cannot account for the panel effects that we have observed. What matters for purposes of the outcomes is the inclinations of judges on the panel (informed as they are by the litigants). It is because of these inclinations that the existence of a unified, rather than divided, panel can make all the difference.

Note in this regard that for the polarization hypothesis to hold, it is not necessary to know whether judges spend a great deal of time offering reasons to one another, or even discussing the issues of all. Mere exposure to a conclusion is enough.[30] A system of simple votes unaccompanied by reasons should incline judges to polarize. Of course, polarization is more likely, and likely to be larger, if reasons are offered and if discussions occur. No one doubts that reasons, if they are good ones, are likely to make those votes especially persuasive.

Can our general claim of group polarization be squared with our particular finding that ideological amplification does not occur in cases involving abortion and capital punishment (and possibly gay and lesbian rights)? Indeed it can. In those areas, views are largely entrenched, and hence amplification will not occur. If people know what they think, they are less likely to be moved by new arguments, social influences, or corroboration. Where judges show neither dampening nor amplification, the reason is that the various pressures that produce panel influences do not affect them, simply because their views are so firm.

### The Whistleblower Effect

Imagine that existing law is not entirely clear, but that fairly applied, it is best taken to require one or another outcome. It is easily imaginable that like-minded judges, unaccompanied by a potential dissenter, will fail to apply the law as they should. This is not because they are lawless or indifferent to what the law requires. It is because when the law is unclear, fallible human beings might well be inclined to understand the law in a way that fits with their predilections and commitments.

These points provide an additional explanation for some of the differences between divided panels and those in which all judges were appointed by a president of the same political party. Consider affirmative action cases. In some of these cases, three Democratic appointees might well be inclined to vote in favor of validating affirmative action programs even if existing doctrine argues against them. If no Republican appointee is on the panel, there is a risk that the panel will unanimously support validating an affirmative action program despite existing law. The effect of the Republican appointee is to call the panel's attention to the tension between its inclination and the decided cases.

Of course, her efforts might fail. Her co-panelists might persist in their views, perhaps with the claim that those cases can be distinguished. But when existing law does create serious problems for the panel, the presence of a judge with a different inclination might well have a large effect. We speculate that in the areas in which there is a large difference between two-to-one majorities and three judges from the same party, this effect—the whistleblower effect—is playing a role.[31] In short, ideological amplification comes when there is no whistleblower. The whistleblower effect might be understood quite broadly. The easiest cases are those in which existing law actually requires a particular result. But in other cases, the whistleblower can draw her colleagues' attention to legally relevant arguments that, while not necessarily decisive, deserve careful consideration and sometimes make a difference to the outcome.

Most of our data do not allow this speculation to be tested directly, but a separate study shows the importance of a potential dissenter, or whistleblower, in ensuring that courts follow the law.[32] More particularly, a Democratic appointee on a majority Republican court of appeals panel has sometimes turned out to be extremely important in ensuring that such a panel does what the law asks it to do. The basic point is that diversity of view can help to correct errors—not that judges of one or another party are more likely, as such, to be correct.

To understand this study, some background is in order. Under the Supreme Court's decision in *Chevron U.S.A. v. Natural Resources Defense Council*, courts should uphold agency interpretations of law so long as the interpretations do not clearly violate congressional instructions and are "reasonable."[33] But when do courts actually uphold agency interpretations? Existing law allows judges considerable room to maneuver, so that courts that are inclined to invalidate agency interpretations often can find a plausible basis for doing so. The real question is when they will claim to have found that plausible basis.

The relevant study, extending well beyond environmental protection to regulation in general, confirms the idea that party affiliation has an exceedingly large influence on outcomes within the D.C. Circuit. If observers were to code cases very crudely by taking account of whether industry or a public interest group is bringing the challenge, they would find that a panel with a majority of Democratic appointees reaches a liberal judgment 68 percent of the time, whereas a panel with a majority of Republican appointees reaches such a judgment only 46 percent of the time.[34] These findings are broadly in line with our own, larger data set, involving the NLRB, the EPA, and the FCC (see chapter 2).

For present purposes, the most important finding is the dramatic difference between politically diverse panels, with judges appointed by presidents of more than one party, and politically unified panels, with judges appointed by presidents of only one party. On *divided* panels in which a Republican majority of the court might be expected to be hostile to the agency, the court nonetheless upholds the agency's interpretation 62 percent of the time. But on *unified* all-Republican panels, which might be expected to be hostile to the agency, the court upholds the agency's interpretation only 33 percent of the time. Note that this was the only unusual finding in the data. When Democratic majority courts are expected to uphold the agency's decision on political grounds, they do so over 70 percent of the time, whether unified (71 percent of the time) or divided (84 percent of the time). Consider the results in tabular form:[35]

| | RRR panel | RRD panel | RDD panel | DDD panel |
|---|---|---|---|---|
| Invalidate agency action when expected to do so on political grounds | 67 percent | 38 percent | 16 percent | 29 percent |

It is reasonable to speculate that the only seemingly bizarre result—a 67 percent invalidation rate when Republican appointees are unified—reflects group influences and, in particular, group polarization. A group of all-Republican appointees might

well take the relatively unusual step of rejecting an agency's interpretation. By contrast, a divided panel, with a built-in check on
any tendency toward the unusual or extreme outcome, is more
likely to take the conventional route of simply upholding the
agency's action. An important reason may well be that the single
Democratic appointee acts as a whistleblower, discouraging the
other judges from making a decision that is inconsistent with the
Supreme Court's command that courts of appeals should uphold
agency interpretations of ambiguous statutes.[36]

Our own analysis of judicial review of decisions by the FCC,
NLRB, and EPA shows a related pattern.[37] On divided panels,
including at least one Republican or Democratic appointee, we
find little role for politics or party in judicial review of agency
interpretations of law. If the panel consist of two Republican
appointees and one Democratic appointee, or two Democratic
appointees and one Republican appointee, it does not much matter whether the agency decision was made under a Republican or
Democratic president. And when the panel is divided, the rate of
deference to the agency is not much affected by whether the
agency's decision was liberal or conservative.

But things are altogether different on unified panels. All-
Democratic panels are more favorable to Democratic administrations than to Republican administrations. They are also more
favorable to liberal decisions than to conservative ones. All-
Republican panels show the opposite tendency. They are more
likely to uphold the decisions of Republican administrations,
and they show a definite tendency to favor conservative rulings
over liberal ones. It is not unreasonable to speculate that the
whistleblower effect accounts for the apparent neutrality of
divided panels—and for the strikingly political behavior of unified panels.

We do not know whether the whistleblower effect accounts for many areas of the law in which judges show far more moderation on divided panels than on unified ones. To answer that question, it would be helpful not merely to collect and count votes, but also to investigate the substance behind the relevant area of law. But it is certainly reasonable to speculate that, some of the time, ideological amplification results from the simple absence of a whistleblower.

## Why Aren't the Effects Larger?

We have been emphasizing the existence of strong party and panel effects. But this is only part of the story, and there is another way of reading the evidence. It would be possible to see our data as a real tribute to the rule of law—as suggesting that, most of the time, the law is what matters, not party or ideology. Even when party effects are significant, they are not overwhelmingly large. Recall that Republican appointees cast stereotypically liberal votes 40 percent of the time, whereas Democratic appointees do so 52 percent of the time. Nearly half of the votes of Democratic appointees are stereotypically conservative, and two-fifths of the votes of Republican appointees are stereotypically liberal!

More often than not, Republican and Democratic appointees agree with one another, even in the most controversial cases, which are our focus here. The rule of law seems to work in the sense that party differences do not have anything like the same kind of effects that they seem to have in the domain of politics generally. Why is this?

We think that the answer has three parts. The first consists of panel effects. Republican appointees often sit with one or more Democratic appointees, and Democratic appointees often sit with one or more Republican appointees. If judges are influenced by one another, the random assignment of judges will inevitably produce some dampening of differences, simply because most panels are divided. To the extent that panels are unified—a likelier event in periods in which a large majority of judges have been appointed by presidents of a single party—we would expect to see much larger party differences.

The second factor involves the disciplining effect of precedent and law—a factor that might be labeled "professionalism" (what we earlier described as binding law). If the law imposes serious constraints, judges will reach the same result whatever their inclinations. Judges are not exactly umpires; they have a great deal of discretion. (True, umpires sometimes have discretion too.) But some of the time, the law will dictate or strongly favor one or another result. In the context of Commerce Clause challenges to legislation, for example, we have explained judicial agreement across party lines partly on the ground that precedent is generally seen to dispose of most current disputes. Sometimes precedent will allow some, but not much, space for ideological differences to emerge. Undoubtedly, the large measure of agreement is partly a product of the constraints of law itself.

In some areas, those constraints will increase agreement between Republican and Democratic appointees. In other areas, they will permit disagreement, but they will discipline its magnitude. And when the law is genuinely binding, judges will be disciplined, whatever the party of the appointing president. The role of the Supreme Court is exceedingly important here. When the Court has been clear, there will be no room for disagreement between lower court appointees of different political parties.

The third factor involves legal and political culture. For all of their differences, Democratic and Republican judicial appointees are rarely ideologues or extremists. If a sex-discrimination plaintiff presents a strong claim, almost all Republican appointees will agree with her, even if the law allows judges to exercise discretion.

If industry is able to show that an environmental regulation is plainly arbitrary, almost all Democratic appointees will strike it down as arbitrary, even if the law would allow them to uphold it. The process of legal training imposes strong limits on what judges seek to do. Judges do not simply vote their political convictions.

There is a related point. The political culture constrains presidential appointments in multiple ways. By virtue of the democratic process, most presidents will usually want to appoint judges whose views fall within a specified range of reasonable convictions. Of course, presidents can greatly differ across party lines, but candidates are not likely to be elected if they would seek judges who fall outside of an identifiable range. For example, President Clinton was widely regarded as a liberal president on many issues, but at least as a general rule, he did not want to appoint extremely liberal judges. President George W. Bush is widely regarded as a quite conservative president, but few of his appointees have been wildly or exceptionally conservative. Some people might quibble with these statements; what counts as extremely liberal, or exceptionally conservative, is in the eye of the beholder. But the important point is the general one. For any democratically elected president, there is a range of acceptable views, and those who do not fall within the range will not be appointed. As a result, the differences between Republican and Democratic appointees will be smaller than might be anticipated.

Even if presidents sometimes seek to appoint extremists, the political process will ensure a kind of filtering that will, to a substantial extent, prevent presidents from nominating (and the Senate from confirming) people whose views are perceived as extreme. Presidents anticipate public concern and outrage, and an appointee who is thought to be extreme might well produce a large public reaction. Under both Democratic and Republican presidents, the Senate has been willing to take a strong stand against nominees perceived as "too liberal" or "too conservative."

We do not mean to say anything controversial here about what most presidents seek to do, or can do. Undoubtedly, a president has more room to maneuver when his party controls the Senate; some of President George W. Bush's more controversial nominees were confirmed because his party had a large majority. Our only point is that the high levels of agreement between Republican and Democratic appointees are undoubtedly affected by political constraints on the choice of federal judges. Insofar as our evidence shows less in the way of party effects than some people might expect, professional discipline and legal consensus help to explain the level of agreement.

## Judicial Ideology and the Rule of Law

The effort to explain our key findings is now complete. Notwithstanding significant party and panel effects, our findings can be seen as a tribute to the rule of law. When party does not matter, it is either because the law imposes real limits on what judges can do, or because judges agree on the underlying questions of value. In the areas of abortion and capital punishment, party matters but panel does not; the explanation lies in the fact that many judges' views are entrenched and hence impervious to panel effects.

Ideological dampening can be found in the numerous areas in which Democratic appointees sitting with two Republican appointees show relatively conservative voting patterns—and in which Republican appointees sitting with two Democratic appointees show relatively liberal voting patterns. We have explained this result by reference to the collegial concurrence. This is a kind of conformity effect, establishing that to a large extent, federal judges behave like ordinary people in psychology experiments. Collegial concurrences are part of everyday experience; they also play a significant role within the federal judiciary. Sometimes judges defer to the views of their colleagues; sometimes they believe that it is not worthwhile to dissent even if they disagree. But we have also noted that judicial conformists may have a significant effect on the drafting of the opinion.

Our most dramatic finding is ideological amplification, by which both Republican and Democratic appointees show relatively extreme ideological tendencies on unified panels. We have explained this finding by reference to group polarization—the pervasive process that leads like-minded people to go to extremes. Here, too, federal judges act in a way that accords with social science experiments on human behavior. The exchange of conclusions and reasons undoubtedly helps to explain why judges show a greater tendency toward ideological voting when sitting with two other appointees of a president of the same political party. We have established this point by reference to outcomes; an investigation of opinions and rationales would probably show that we have understated the effect of group polarization on the federal bench.

# The Case of Big Decisions

# 5

## Of Segregation, Abortion, and Obscenity

T hus far, our picture of judicial behavior has been relatively static. We have not examined changes over time. But it is natural to wonder whether ideological agreements might grow or dampen over long periods. A great deal of evidence suggests that splits between Republican and Democratic appointees were much smaller before the 1970s, in part because the appointment process was much less politicized, at least within the lower courts.[1] For much of the nation's history, lower court appointments were greatly influenced by senators in the relevant home state, and the senatorial role reduced the effects of ideology. And in key areas of the law, casual empiricism suggests that disagreements have intensified in the last decades. In areas involving abortion and discrimination, for example, splits between Democratic and Republican appointees seem to have become especially dramatic.

In this chapter, we study temporal change by exploring a single question, one that we find particularly intriguing: Within the courts of appeals, what happens in the aftermath of a major ruling from the Supreme Court? It is possible to imagine various possibilities. Perhaps major rulings sharply discipline the lower courts by eliminating disagreements across Republican and Democratic appointees. But perhaps such rulings intensify such disagreements by spurring new controversies that will predictably cause ideological conflict.

We focus here on the influence of major Supreme Court decisions in three of the most controversial areas of constitutional law: racial segregation, abortion, and obscenity. The first two areas are obvious choices. When the Supreme Court struck down segregation in 1954, and when it protected the right to choose abortion in 1973, it created an immense public outcry—and it also spurred a great deal of litigation. The area of obscenity is a less obvious choice, but two major decisions dominate the field, and a large number of controversies followed in the wakes of those decisions.

As we shall see, all three areas reveal the same basic pattern: In the immediate aftermath of a major ruling by the Supreme Court, the difference between Democratic and Republican appointees is sharply dampened, apparently because the legal system is working to ensure conformity with the Court's ruling. As time goes on, however, and as new issues arise, the difference grows. One likely reason is that the larger meaning of the major decisions becomes contested as new litigants agree on its "core"; disputes over that larger meaning split Democratic and Republican appointees. Note that we are only testing the impact of Supreme Court decisions on lower court decisions that follow them; we are not offering a "before and after" picture of lower court rulings, testing how such rulings look prior to and after a Supreme Court ruling. Such a picture would undoubtedly be valuable. Our inquiry here involves a different puzzle, which is whether Democratic and

Republican appointees react differently over time in the aftermath of large cases.

## Segregation by Race

*Brown* v. *Board of Education*[2] was the landmark 1954 case in which the Supreme Court overturned *Plessy* v. *Ferguson*[3] and repudiated the "separate but equal" doctrine. The decision created an immediate and intense public controversy, much of it focused on efforts to enforce the Court's ruling.[4] To explore the effect of the decision on ideological disagreements within the lower courts, we assembled a total of 314 segregation cases from 1945 to 1985 and grouped them into three time periods: 1945–1965, 1966–75, and 1976–85 (see figure 5-1).

In chapter 2, we outlined the data as a whole and we found evidence of both party and panel effects. By disaggregating the data by time period, we are able to see some complexities and shifts in the data—and in particular, the growing difference between Republican and Democratic appointees over time.

### Period 1: 1945–65

In cases between 1945 and 1965, there is no evidence of ideological voting. In the most controversial area of constitutional law, there was no disagreement between Republican and Democratic appointees in the very period in which the controversy was most intense. In that period, Republican appointees vote against segregation 65 percent of the time, while Democratic appointees vote against segregation 67 percent of the time. There is no panel effect at all for Democratic appointees. There is a small hint of a panel effect only among Republican appointees, but it does not even approach statistical significance. Overall then, in this initial

Figure 5-1. *Desegregation Panel Effects, 1945–85*

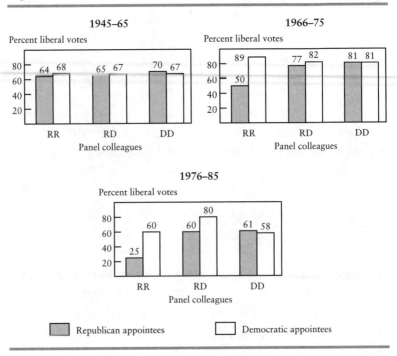

period of desegregation cases (the decades immediately before and after *Brown*), there are no differences among judges appointed by different parties.

*Period 2: 1966–75*

In cases between 1966 and 1975, we find a hint of ideological voting: Overall, Democratic appointees vote against segregation 83 percent of the time, and Republican appointees do so 77 percent of the time.[5] But this difference is relatively small and lacks statistical significance; moreover, it is concentrated in cases in which at least one of the other two panel members was a Republican appointee. Indeed, when the other two members contain no

Republican appointees, the party difference vanishes. Hence we find essentially no difference between Republican and Democratic appointees, not only in the nine years before *Brown*, but also in the twenty-one years after the Court's ruling.

In addition, we see an amplification of the pattern suggested in the early period: no panel effect for Democratic appointees, but a discernible panel effect for Republican appointees, one that approaches statistical significance ($p = .19$).[6] Republican appointees show some ideological dampening: A Republican appointee sitting with two Democratic appointees votes against segregation 81 percent of the time. The most striking number here involves unified Republican panels: A Republican appointee sitting with two other Republicans votes against segregation only 50 percent of the time—far less than the 79 percent rate when sitting with at least one Democrat on the panel.

### Period 3: 1976–85

In this final period, between 1966 and 1975, we see a mature version of the pattern that begins in the first period and grows to a hint in the second period. Overall, Democratic appointees vote against segregation 68 percent of the time, and Republican appointees do so 52 percent of the time, a difference that is now significant ($p < .05$). The difference is again concentrated in cases where at least one of the other two panel members is a Republican appointee. We also see no panel effect for Democratic appointees, but a statistically significant panel effect for Republican appointees ($p < .05$). Republican appointees also show ideological amplification: A Republican appointee sitting on an all-Republican panel votes against segregation only 25 percent of the time. Thus, both party and panel effects increase substantially during the final period, in which the nation was highly ambivalent about "busing" remedies for school segregation.

Figure 5-2. *Abortion Panel Effects, 1971–2005*

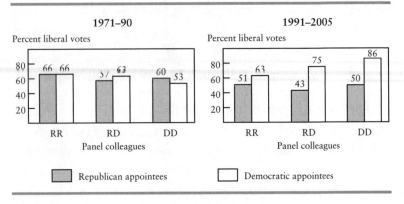

Abortion

In the 1973 decision of *Roe* v. *Wade*, the Supreme Court declared that abortion is a fundamental right guaranteed by the Due Process Clause.[7] In chapter 2, we observed the abortion data overall and found evidence of party effects but no panel effects. To explore *Roe*'s impact on lower court rulings over time, we now disaggregate the abortion data into two time periods: 1971–90 and 1991–2005 (see figure 5-2). As we shall see, the question of abortion shows a similarly growing split between Republican and Democratic appointees.

*Period 1: 1971–90*

It is striking to see that between 1971 and 1990 there are no party effects: Democratic appointees cast a pro-choice vote 62 percent of the time, and Republican appointees do so 58 percent of the time.[8] There are also no panel effects for either party. During this period, the ideological affiliation of the appointing president does not matter in the abortion context. This is a surprising finding, to which we shall return. Perhaps the two parties did not greatly disagree, and their consensus was reflected in judicial voting patterns. Or perhaps *Roe* was taken to settle the law, in a way that temporarily eliminated the relevance of conflicts between the two sets of appointees.

### Period 2: 1991–2005

In cases between 1991 and 2005, there is powerful evidence of ideological voting: Republican appointees cast a pro-choice vote 46 percent of the time, while Democratic appointees cast a pro-choice vote 72 percent of the time. The 26 percent difference is exceedingly large—among the largest in our entire data set ($p < .001$).

In this period, there is no overall panel effect. But when we disaggregate, we find that while Republican appointees revealed no panel effects, Democratic appointees do show a statistically significant panel effect ($p < .05$). Among Democratic appointees, we find ideological dampening: A Democratic appointee sitting with two Republican appointees casts a pro-choice vote 63 percent of the time. Among Democratic appointees, we also find evidence of ideological amplification: A Democratic appointee sitting with two other Democratic appointees cast a pro-choice vote a remarkable 86 percent of the time.

## Obscenity

The debate over restrictions on sexually explicit materials has been among the most heated in all of free speech law. In chapter 2, we noted that in this area there is solid evidence of both ideological voting and panel effects. How has judicial behavior changed over time?

In this area, two Supreme Court decisions have proven particularly important in organizing the constitutional inquiry: *Roth* v.

Figure 5-3. *Obscenity Panel Effects, 1958–2005*

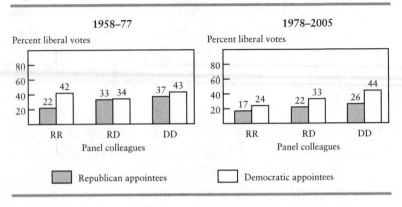

1958–77

Percent liberal votes

| | RR | RD | DD |
|---|---|---|---|
| Republican appointees | 22 | 33 | 37 |
| Democratic appointees | 42 | 34 | 43 |

Panel colleagues

1978–2005

Percent liberal votes

| | RR | RD | DD |
|---|---|---|---|
| Republican appointees | 17 | 22 | 26 |
| Democratic appointees | 24 | 33 | 44 |

Panel colleagues

☐ Republican appointees          ☐ Democratic appointees

*United States*[9] and *Miller* v. *California.*[10] *Roth* held that obscene material was not protected by the First Amendment when the underlying material was "utterly without redeeming social importance."[11] *Miller* set the modern standard for obscenity regulation, by eliminating the word "utterly" and instructing courts to pay attention to contemporary community standards.[12] We consider the data over two periods: 1958–77 and 1978–2005 (see figure 5-3).

*Period 1: 1958–77*

In obscenity cases between 1958 and 1977, there is some evidence of ideological voting: Republican appointees vote for defendants 30 percent of the time, and Democratic appointees vote for defendants 37 percent of the time.[13] There is also suggestive evidence of panel effects on the Republican side, and in the predicted direction (although not significant). A Republican appointee sitting with two Democratic appointees votes for a defendant 37 percent of the time; the numbers are 22 percent on three-judge Republican panels, and 33 percent on two-judge Republican majority panels.

*Period 2: 1978–2005*

In this later period (1978–2005) obscenity matures into a typical ideological case category, with both large party and panel effects.[14] There is clear evidence of ideological voting: A Republican appointee votes for an obscenity defendant 21 percent of the time, while a Democratic appointee votes for a defendant 32 percent of the time.

We also find evidence of panel effects. Republican appointees showed ideological dampening: A Republican appointee sitting with two Democratic appointees issues a pro-defendant vote 26 percent of the time. Republican appointees also show ideological amplification: A Republican appointee sitting on a three-judge Republican panel issues a pro-defendant ruling only 17 percent of the time. Democratic appointees show the same pattern. A Democratic appointee sitting with two other Democratic appointees issues a pro-defendant ruling 44 percent of the time, with a corresponding rate of 24 percent when sitting with two Republican appointees.

## Party and Panel Effects over Time

### The Basic Pattern

From this investigation, clear patterns emerge. First, in each of the three areas, party effects and panel effects differ across periods, and when they exist, they are in the predicted direction. Second and more notably, all case types show an aggregate increase in both party and panel effects over time. Figure 5-4 displays this pattern.

### Party Effects: Explanations

For each area, we see relatively small party effects in the first time period and comparatively larger ones in the last time period. Why is this? We suggest three possible explanations.

Figure 5-4. *Party and Panel Effects over Time in Desegregation, Abortion, and Obscenity Cases*

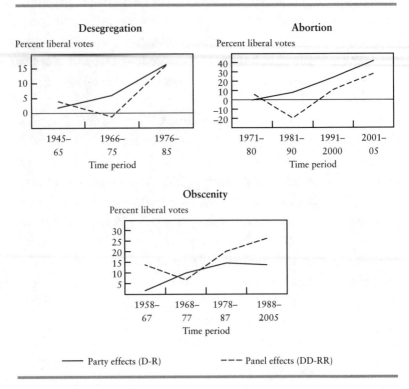

The first is that in the immediate aftermath of a major decision, the lower courts are heavily disciplined by definition, and the legal system is working largely to ensure compliance with the Supreme Court's ruling. On this view, litigants take some time to "catch up" with the Court's instruction, and a number of cases test whether the legal system is really prepared to require people to comply with what the Court has said. In the immediate aftermath of *Brown*, for example, many cases tested the question whether segregation was in fact lawful; lower courts insisted that the Court's ruling really was law. But as years pass, the question is no longer whether the initial decision means what it appears to say. It is instead what the decision means. At that point, ideological disagreements are likely to become more intense. Another way to put the point is to suggest that immediately after a big decision, the legal system must insist on, or at most establish, its "core" meaning. As time goes by, the core is settled, and everyone agrees on it; sharp disputes break out about the implications of the decision for problems that do not lie within the core.

It is easy to see, for example, that fifteen years after *Brown* novel debates began, and these debates were not clearly settled by *Brown* itself. The debates raised questions about the state's obligation to impose aggressive "busing" remedies; the legal status of de facto rather than de jure segregation, that is, segregation produced by apparently voluntary housing decisions; the possibility of desegregation decrees in the North; and the permissibility of pursuing desegregation by involving areas that had not themselves segregated students by race. It is also easy to see that in the years after *Roe*, lower courts were confronted with a range of knotty and novel issues about permissible limitations on the abortion right—involving, for example, spousal and parental consent and the claim that the right to choose abortion also entailed a right to government funding of the choice. The novel issues, not evidently questioning the decision itself, are a predictable source of ideological differences.

We believe that there is a good deal to this explanation for the observed patterns. But the explanation faces an obvious problem: Why do litigants fail to adjust immediately? If litigants are rational, they should so adjust—and if they did, all the cases in the courts of appeals, not simply the later ones, would be genuinely difficult. A natural answer is that the legal system suffers, some of the time, from a certain "lag"—as reflected by the fact that challenges to both segregation and abortion restrictions succeeded well over 60 percent of time in the period after the Court's big decisions.

A second possibility is that in the early periods on which we focus, the federal judiciary was much less divided than it has been in more recent years. In the period between 1945 and 1965, the Democratic Party included both liberal northerners and pro-segregation southerners. In light of senatorial courtesy, ensuring a role for senators in judicial appointments, it should be no surprise that Democratic appointees did not show more liberal voting patterns, in that period, than Republican appointees. More generally, a great deal of evidence supports the general claim that significant splits between Republican and Democratic appointees on the lower courts are a product of the last thirty-five years.[15] This evidence is enough to explain why in the earlier periods, ideological disagreements were less intense with respect to segregation, abortion, and obscenity.

To the extent that this explanation is correct, our data should not be taken to suggest a universal pattern in the aftermath of big decisions; it would therefore be a mistake to think that this pattern will hold in all times and places. We might be finding instead a more particular trend, in the United States over the past decades, toward greater divisions among Republican and Democratic appointees. Our own data cannot exclude the possibility that this explanation is, in fact, the dominant one. Of course, ideological differences on the Supreme Court are as old as the Republic. But perhaps the differences that we observe, on the lower courts, are largely a product of a more recently polarized process.

The third possibility is that the increasing intensity of disagreement along party lines is best understood as an artifact of a similar shift, on the relevant issues, in the country at large. Initially, Democrats and Republicans may not greatly disagree on an issue; but changing events and values, and a dramatic Supreme

Court ruling in particular, may polarize the parties. After the polarization has occurred, judicial views are likely to be affected, in part as a result of the nomination and confirmation process itself. On this view, the Court's decisions helped to unleash the very political forces that produced a more polarized judiciary.

Before *Roe*, for example, the question of abortion did not split Republicans and Democrats in general. In the 1950s and 1960s, abortion was not a nationally salient issue, and it would be hard to say that the leaders of the Republican Party were more pro-life than the leaders of the Democratic Party. And prior to *Roe*, a Democratic president would not have screened out potential nominees who did not support a woman's right to choose. A Republican president would have been similarly unconcerned about the nominee's likely views on the abortion question. On this view, the recent increase in party differences reflects a change in the country, one that was spurred in large part by the Court itself and later reflected in the views of judges. Note that this explanation, unlike the second, does not rely on a more general trend toward a more polarized judiciary. It relies in particular on the polarization with respect to the three issues at hand.

The segregation data can be understood in similar terms. In 1954 there was no simple split between Republicans and Democrats on the issue of segregation. The split divided regions much more than it did parties. To be sure, the civil rights movement had a distinctive influence on the Johnson administration in particular, and hence racial issues did play a role in national political divisions in the 1960s. But the division over desegregation orders intensified with Richard Nixon's criticism of intrusive "busing remedies" in the 1968 campaign. After his election, President Nixon appointed Supreme Court justices who tended to take a more cautious approach to such remedies, and the views of Republican nominees in general apparently showed a similar caution. The pattern is not identical to what is observed in the context of abortion, but here as well, the Court's decision helped to set in motion certain forces that ultimately produced polarization within the lower courts.

The obscenity data are much harder to explain in these terms, simply because the Court's decisions did not have nearly the same degree of political salience as those in the context of segregation and abortion. But by giving constitutional protection to sexually explicit speech, the Court did contribute to the view that the federal judiciary is an important location for the "culture wars," in which both Republican and Democratic leaders have a large stake. To be sure, no president appoints judges solely or mostly because of their views on obscenity. But after the Court's decisions, and the continuing public debate of which they are a part, the constitutional status of sexually explicit speech has become a question on which Republican and Democratic nominees frequently divide.

### Panel Effects: Explanations

We also find increasing panel effects over time. This, too, might seem to be a puzzle. But each of the explanations for party effects probably accounts for increased panel effects as well. If party effects are small, panel effects should be small too; and hence an intensification of panel effects should be expected as party effects grow. As we will see in the next chapter, there is a general correspondence between the size of party and panel effects across different circuits as well.

This account is strengthened if we recall the mechanisms underlying group polarization. Begin with the early period after a decision, in which one important task is to ensure compliance. If there are no party effects, there are unlikely to be panel effects. But suppose that in some areas of the country, Republican appointees were slightly more sympathetic, in the period around *Brown*, to segregation than were Democratic appointees. Even if this were so, persuasive arguments, in the period between 1954 and 1965, would be unlikely to fuel polarization and hence amplification. Because the issues were so new, the available arguments were few and sparse. The central question was how to ensure desegregation, not how to understand complications and complexities.

Compare the latter periods, when judges, litigants, and academics will have argued a great deal about the meaning and reach of the Court's decision. Republican and Democratic appointees will have a much larger available "stock" of arguments pointing in different directions. Many fresh claims will have been developed—and polarization will therefore become more likely. And as liberals and conservatives separate into two sets of views, corroboration may be expected to play a larger role. Hence it should be no surprise to see growing panel effects at the same time that party effects intensify.

Of course, it is theoretically possible to have large party effects with small or no panel effects; some of the data with respect to abortion show this possibility. But as a general pattern, the two sets of effects march hand-in-hand.

### Overall Voting Patterns over Time

What accounts for changing percentages of liberal voting? Why do those patterns not remain constant? Why do they ebb and flow?

It might be tempting to speculate that after *Brown* the rate of liberal votes would be extremely high. In 1955, after all, segregation was plainly unlawful; perhaps judges should show a 100 percent voting rate "against segregation." But this is not what the evidence shows. The period immediately following *Brown*—from

1955 to 1965—reveals a 66 percent overall liberal voting rate. The jump in liberal voting did not occur in the period immediately following *Brown*; it occurred ten years later. Between 1966 and 1975, the liberal voting rate increased and peaked; 81 percent of judges' votes during that time period opposed segregation. During the following period (1976–85) the number drops back to 61 percent, which is not statistically different from the immediate post-decision period (see above). In fact, the Republican liberal voting rate during 1966–75 (77 percent) is higher than the overall Democratic voting rate over the full 1945–85 period (74 percent).

*Roe* might also be expected to have an immediate and strong liberalizing effect on the law—and in an obvious sense it did, simply because it created a broad right to choose. Something of this general sort is reflected in our data as well. Between 1971 and 1980 (encompassing two years before *Roe*), the overall liberal voting percentage is at 70 percent. But in the next ten year period, from 1981–90, 52 percent of judges' votes are liberal. Though the liberal percentage increases in the 1991–2000 period to 60 percent, it has subsequently fallen to 47 percent in the 2001–04 period.

The obscenity data are more complicated still, in part because there are two major cases to absorb, rather than one. *Roth*, decided in 1957, might be expected to have an immediate and substantial liberalizing impact on the law. But the 1958–67 period had a 32 percent liberal voting rate; the 1968–77 period was nearly identical at 34 percent. In the 1978–87 period, however, the liberal voting rate dropped to 21 percent before rebounding in the 1988–2005 period to 36 percent. *Miller*, decided in 1973, was a somewhat more conservative ruling than *Roth*, but it did not move voting rates in any discernible direction.

How can these trends be explained? The first point involves selection effects. It is wrong to think that the rate of liberal votes must increase significantly after a liberal decision, simply because the mix of cases will not remain the same. After *Brown*, people will not litigate the same cases that they litigated before. It is therefore far too simple to say that after *Brown*, 100 percent of votes should be expected to be "against segregation." In the ten years after that decision, litigants will often raise questions and problems that *Brown* did not explicitly resolve. In the context of segregation, of course, there was a high degree of intransigence, in which courts were simply asked to enforce the desegregation mandate. But in some of the relevant cases, the nature of the mandate was not entirely clear. After any big decision, the new mix of cases, adjusting to what the Court has said, will mean that there may be no shift in the direction of more liberal or more conservative voting.

Indeed, we might be tempted to expect that in many areas of law, the rate of liberal votes would remain constant over time. As a rough first approximation, it might be expected that rational litigants will adjust to the point that the range of liberal outcomes remains in the general vicinity of 50 percent (a point to which we return in the next chapter). But selection effects merely raise a further puzzle: Why do we see different patterns over time? Why is the rate of liberal decisions not consistently in the range of 50 percent—which is what might be expected if litigation is limited to those cases that are genuinely difficult after the big decision?

If we focus on the numbers in the immediate aftermath of the Court's *Brown* decision, one possibility has to do with the particular dynamic of segregation. As we have intimated, flagrant violations of *Brown* persisted in the real world, and some institutions with segregation schemes simply refused to come into compliance after the decision.[16] A form of civil disobedience certainly contributed to the numbers for segregation. The relatively high rate of liberal votes in the decade after *Brown* might well reflect the continuing existence of easy cases. But why did the rate of liberal votes, in the context of segregation, actually *increase* in the decade after the decision? A likely possibility is that the federal judiciary as a whole might well have shifted to the left, in general and on the particular question of segregation—perhaps because of the growing number of Democratic appointees (by Presidents Kennedy and Johnson), perhaps because of a broader shift in judicial sentiment. In the early years after *Brown*, some judges may have been resistant to the Supreme Court's decision. At the very least, they were willing to provide extended time for compliance.[17] In the context of segregation, early conservative votes, including those from Democratic appointees, might be attributable to this resistance.

On this view, the true lessons of *Brown* were not fully or willingly absorbed by those sitting on courts of appeals at the time of the decision. Instead, it was only those judges appointed later, Republican and perhaps particularly Democratic, who understood what the case meant and were able to apply it faithfully. This explanation is complemented by the existence, in the context of school segregation, of a series of Supreme Court decisions that firmly underlined and even extended the reach of *Brown*.[18] In the immediate aftermath of *Brown*, some judges did not insist on desegregation—and the persistence of unlawful segregation, alongside the appointment of judges intent on eliminating it, contributed to a growing rate of liberal decisions in the late 1960s and early 1970s. In a way, this point complements one we made earlier: Just as a big decision can set in motion the very forces that produce later polarization, so too such a decision may set in motion forces that ultimately embrace the decision, and produce enthusiasm for its enforcement and even extension.

In all three areas, we have also seen a reversion to moderate voting patterns in later periods. *Roe* is the most dramatic example. The decision was followed by a high rate of liberal voting in abortion cases—70 percent in the ten years following the decision. But by 2001–04, that rate dropped to 47 percent. For segregation and obscenity, the pattern is broadly similar. Why do we see decreased rates of liberal votes over time?

The best explanation of this phenomenon pays attention to three key factors: selection effects, new guidance from the Supreme Court, and changes in the composition of the courts. The abortion problem might be taken as exemplary. With respect to selection effects, the mix of cases unquestionably adjusted to Court's ruling in *Roe*. After 1992, it has been exceedingly rare for litigants to try to challenge *Roe* directly. The core of the decision was reaffirmed in that year,[19] and hence pro-life advocates were unlikely to challenge the abortion right as such. The actual cases raised the difficult and more technical question whether certain restrictions imposed an "undue burden" on the relevant right.[20] The Supreme Court had given a clear signal that it would accept some restrictions on the abortion right—more restrictions, in fact, than *Roe* itself had appeared to allow.[21] For this reason, pro-choice votes were hardly inevitable under the new doctrine. A higher rate of conservative votes was invited by the Court's shifting guidance. Finally, and significantly, the lower courts were almost certainly more conservative in the early twenty-first century than in the 1970s—in general and on the question of abortion in particular. With a larger percentage of Republican appointees, and with greater attention to the abortion issue among political conservatives, the federal judiciary should be expected to be more receptive to restrictions on the abortion right. Of course, litigants should adjust accordingly. But if selection effects, new guidance, and the changing judiciary are taken together, a decreased rate of liberal votes, in the abortion area, should hardly be surprising.

With segregation and obscenity, these points hold as well. Litigants should be expected to adjust to ideological shifts within the courts, but the adjustment may well take time. To elaborate on these conclusions, we must turn to the next chapter. For now, let us simply underline the patterns that we have observed. In the aftermath of a major decision, the split between Republican and Democratic appointees tends to be muted. That split increases over time, as litigants agree on the "core" meaning of that decision and dispute whether it should be extended or instead qualified. If this pattern is observed in the contexts of segregation, abortion, and obscenity, it will probably be observed in many other areas as well.

# More Conservative than Thou?

## Judicial Voting across Circuits, across Presidents, and over Time

# 6

W e now turn to three large sets of questions. First: Can some courts of appeals be shown to be more liberal than others? Do party and panel effects differ across courts of appeals? Second: Can presidents be ranked in terms of voting patterns of their judicial appointees? Is there a difference between the appointees of, say, President Reagan and President George W. Bush? Third: Is the federal judiciary becoming more liberal or, instead, more conservative over time? As we shall see, these questions are not easy to answer, but it is possible to make some progress on them, and we can learn a great deal from seeing exactly why simple conclusions are unreliable.

## Differences across Circuits

There are twelve federal courts of appeals,[1] and there is a great deal of speculation about which are more conservative and which more liberal. From our data, it is possible to disaggregate the cases by circuit to see whether the effects observed in the overall data hold across the board. To obtain a sense of what is happening across circuits, we aggregated the various cases within circuits.[2] The simplest finding has to do with ideological variations across circuits.

Consider figure 6-1. In accordance with standard lore, the Third and Ninth Circuits are two of the most liberal, and the Seventh and Eighth Circuits are two of the most conservative. The rankings, in terms of ideology, correlate strongly, but not perfectly, with the percentage of Democratic appointees on the relevant court in 2002 ($r = .58$).[3]

Note that the figure, while suggestive, is quite crude in a way that will complicate all of our efforts to test for ideological differences across courts and across time. The fundamental point is that different circuits do not decide the same cases, or even kinds of cases, and hence there is no simple test here of ideological differences. From table 2-1 in chapter 2, it is easy to see that the rate of victory is far higher in some areas than in others. Some circuits will see more cases in which plaintiffs have a great deal of difficulty in prevailing, and the percentage of liberal votes will be affected accordingly. Across circuits, the differing percentages of liberal votes do not result from a carefully controlled experiment.

In some contexts, moreover, litigants are severely constrained in their ability to choose among circuits. For review of some administrative agency decisions, for example, litigants must proceed in the D.C. Circuit; and "venue" limitations often ensure that there is a limited range of choice among courts of appeals. If litigants are restricted to a liberal circuit, or to a conservative one, the mix of cases will be significantly affected, and different circuits will see quite different cases. To this extent, cross-circuit comparisons are not reliable.

A distinctive complication arises when litigants have discretion about where to file. Usually, litigants will not press a case before a court of appeals in which they expect to lose; they will adjust their behavior to the anticipated behavior of the court before which they expect to appear. Those who are complaining of sex discrimination, for example, should "flock" to courts of appeals that are expected to be favorably disposed to their complaints. Indeed, litigants would bring cases before courts that are perceived as liberal that they would not bring before courts perceived as conservative. To the extent that litigants can choose where to bring suit, we might not be surprised if a conservative circuit were to end up with exactly the same percentage of liberal votes as a far more liberal circuit.

But this point actually can be taken to support the overall rankings in figure 6-1, because it suggests that our findings might well *understate* differences among courts of appeals. The ideological gap between the (famously liberal) Ninth Circuit and the (famously conservative) Fourth Circuit is probably greater than the raw numbers suggest, simply because parties are bringing cases in the Ninth Circuit that they would not bring in the Fourth. If the Fourth Circuit shows more conservative voting rates than the Ninth, even though "liberal" cases are less likely to be brought in the former circuit, then there is good reason to believe that the Fourth Circuit is indeed more conservative than the Ninth. Because there is no controlled experiment here, of course, we can offer no assurance that our rankings are reliable. But the figure is certainly suggestive, and it fits well with conventional wisdom about ideological differences across circuits.

Now let us turn to another question, one where more reliable answers are possible: whether the effects of party and panel differ across circuits. As before, to obtain a measure of party effects, we subtract the percentage of liberal votes by Republican appointees

Figure 6-1. *Circuit Court Composition and Individual Voting Patterns*[a]

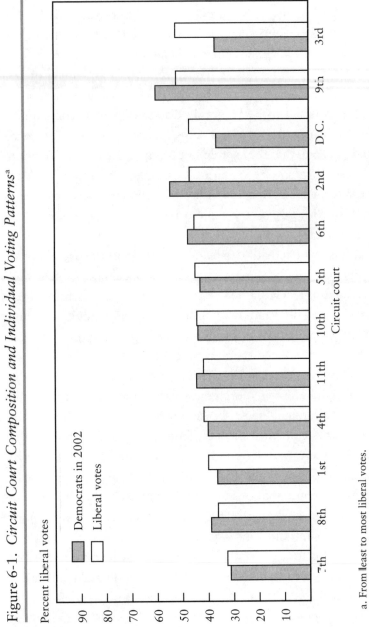

a. From least to most liberal votes.

from the percentage of liberal votes by Democratic appointees; this is a good test for whether party predicts likely votes. To create our measure of panel effects, we subtract the percentage of liberal votes by judges (whether Republican or Democratic) sitting with two Republican appointees from the percentage of such votes of judges sitting with two Democratic appointees. Figure 6-2 presents the results.

The major finding is that there are party differences in all circuits, although they do differ in magnitude. The D.C. Circuit shows small party differences (less than 10 percent), followed by a group of nine circuits with party differences in the 10 percent–20 percent range, followed by the Sixth and Ninth Circuits, which show by far the largest party difference (22 percent and 21 percent, respectively).

Larger party differences also tend to be accompanied by larger panel differences. There is a correlation of .43 between the sizes of party and panel effects. To some extent, party differences are a prerequisite for panel differences, particularly to the extent that the sharing of different perspectives is an important part of what produces panel effects (see chapter 4). If so, then it follows that larger panel differences would come from larger party differences. Interestingly, in nine of the twelve circuits, a judge's vote is predicted fairly well by the political affiliation of the president who appointed the judge in question; and it is predicted at least as well by the political affiliation of the president who appointed the two other panel members. The Sixth Circuit, which has a large party effect but a comparatively small panel effect, is the most significant exception to this pattern. There is also a modest tendency for panel differences to be larger as the ideology of the circuit becomes more liberal (a correlation across circuits of .35 between the percentage of liberal votes and the size of the panel difference). The interpretation of this is not entirely clear, although it

Figure 6-2. *Party and Panel Effects on Individual Judges' Votes, by Circuit Court*[a]

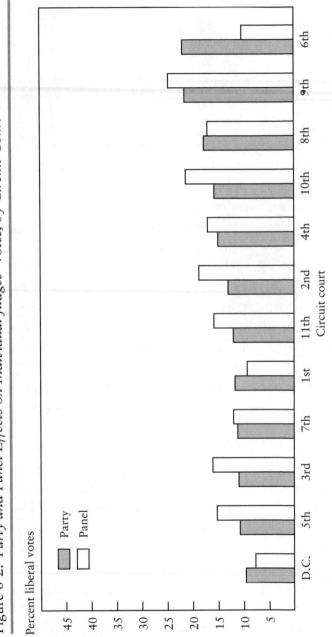

a. From smallest to largest party difference.

may result from the fact that there is a tendency for party differences to be larger in the circuits with a larger percentage of Democratic appointees ($r = .61$ between percent Ds and party difference). Democratic appointees are more susceptible than Republican appointees to panel effects.

## Differences across Presidents

Now let us turn to some larger and more controversial matters. It is natural to wonder whether different presidents can be "ranked" in terms of the ideology of their judicial appointees. By common lore, for example, President Reagan was determined to "stock" the federal bench with conservative judges, whereas President George H. W. Bush was significantly more moderate and President George W. Bush behaved more like President Reagan. Many people think that President Clinton was able, or willing, to appoint only moderately liberal judges. Our data provide a great deal of information about judicial voting behavior under different presidents.

Let us begin with an initial ranking, undertaken in terms of raw percentage of liberal votes across all cases (first row of table 6-1). What is noteworthy about this ranking is that both Democratic and Republican appointees seem to be growing more conservative over time. (If this is indeed the trend, it could be because of shifts within the Supreme Court, rather than within the lower courts; perhaps the Supreme Court is moving lower courts in more conservative directions. In fact, it is possible that the Supreme Court is driving any such shifts; we will return to this issue below.) It would be tempting to take this table as demonstrative of a plausible proposition, which is that appointees of Reagan, Bush I, and Bush II are more conservative than appointees of Nixon and Ford, and that appointees of Clinton

Table 6-1. *Percentage of Liberal Votes by Appointing President and Case Category*[a]

Percent

| | Eisenhower | Kennedy | Johnson | Nixon | Ford | Carter | Reagan | Bush I | Clinton | Bush II |
|---|---|---|---|---|---|---|---|---|---|---|
| All Cases (493) | 56 (256) | 59 (985) | 59 (1,155) | 46 (575) | 44 (2,832) | 54 (5,895) | 39 (2,988) | 36 (3,580) | 48 (198) | 38 |
| Affirmative action | 63 (8) | 73 (11) | 81 (37) | 65 (49) | 55 (29) | 73 (112) | 39 (148) | 46 (41) | 76 (46) | |
| Abortion | 69 (16) | 59 (22) | 62 (50) | 64 (59) | 52 (23) | 65 (84) | 46 (112) | 43 (28) | 79 (38) | 0 (3) |
| Americans with Disabilities Act | 71 (3) | 45 (7) | 43 (89) | 42 (76) | 67 (85) | 36 (314) | 26 (698) | 25 (378) | 27 (564) | 33 (39) |
| Campaign finance | 50 (2) | 50 (2) | 20 (10) | 37 (19) | 25 (4) | 48 (40) | 33 (51) | 19 (32) | 47 (30) | 40 (5) |
| Capital punishment | | 50 (2) | 43 (21) | 14 (14) | 13 (16) | 47 (89) | 21 (217) | 24 (124) | 43 (136) | 0 (5) |
| Contracts | 40 (5) | 50 (4) | 40 (20) | 25 (32) | 33 (12) | 35 (46) | 28 (69) | 8 (26) | 11 (18) | 100 (1) |
| Criminal appeals | 0 (2) | | 34 (91) | 35 (303) | 34 (62) | 38 (494) | 32 (1,335) | 29 (872) | 34 (965) | |
| Environmental Protection Agency | 75 (4) | 50 (6) | 78 (23) | 72 (25) | 38 (8) | 58 (137) | 52 (183) | 39 (66) | 62 (87) | 75 (4) |
| Federalism | 100 (4) | 100 (3) | 97 (38) | 95 (38) | 97 (38) | 95 (147) | 96 (303) | 90 (153) | 99 (219) | 94 (17) |
| Piercing corporate veil | 50 (2) | | 56 (18) | 35 (17) | 15 (13) | 45 (47) | 23 (111) | 29 (58) | 32 (79) | |

| | | | | | | | | | | |
|---|---|---|---|---|---|---|---|---|---|---|
| Sex discrimination | 29 (7) | 29 (7) | 51 (130) | 41 (131) | 43 (131) | 56 (445) | 33 (1,108) | 35 (578) | 51 (669) | 32 (37) |
| Takings | 75 (16) | 75 (16) | 75 (59) | 80 (69) | 75 (32) | 82 (148) | 76 (208) | 76 (66) | 92 (37) | 100 (3) |
| Title 7 | 0 (2) | 0 (3) | 40 (42) | 32 (37) | 45 (40) | 45 (146) | 31 (401) | 40 (181) | 42 (223) | 14 (14) |
| Punitive damages | | 50 (2) | 83 (12) | 70 (10) | 57 (7) | 61 (33) | 75 (83) | 75 (51) | 79 (62) | 75 (4) |
| First amendment | 86 (7) | 60 (5) | 63 (24) | 62 (34) | 60 (15) | 53 (75) | 43 (69) | 56 (34) | 71 (24) | 33 (3) |
| Obscenity | 33 (135) | 28 (46) | 34 (93) | 22 (92) | 21 (14) | 34 (47) | 25 (44) | 22 (9) | 33 (3) | 0 (1) |
| Gay and lesbian rights | 0 (2) | 0 (3) | 0 (2) | 0 (4) | 25 (4) | 60 (10) | 20 (25) | 14 (7) | 88 (8) | |
| National Environmental Policy Act | | 0 (2) | 17 (6) | 27 (11) | 25 (4) | 59 (39) | 25 (60) | 9 (35) | 40 (98) | 17 (18) |
| Desegregation | 66 (274) | 75 (106) | 87 (191) | 61 (110) | 50 (14) | 38 (39) | 40 (5) | | | |
| Standing | 0 (1) | | 17 (6) | 0 (4) | 0 (2) | 56 (189) | 46 (325) | 41 (125) | 38 (110) | |
| Federal Communications Commission | | 80 (5) | 75 (4) | 50 (2) | 25 (4) | 52 (62) | 52 (147) | 51 (51) | 65 (52) | |
| 11th Amendment abrogation | 50 (2) | 33 (3) | 53 (15) | 58 (12) | 69 (13) | 58 (48) | 35 (103) | 33 (48) | 63 (72) | 0 (2) |
| National Labor Relations Board | 0 (1) | 0 (1) | 0 (4) | 43 (7) | 20 (5) | 59 (41) | 36 (90) | 40 (25) | 63 (40) | 100 (2) |

a. Number of votes in parentheses. Blank cells indicate no data available.

are more conservative than appointees of Carter and Johnson. And if the rate of liberal votes is indeed taken as probative, then this judgment is perfectly legitimate.

But it should be immediately apparent that there is a now-familiar problem with this simple ranking exercise: The mix of case types changes over time. The Americans with Disabilities Act (ADA), for example, was enacted in 1990, and since that time the federal courts have faced a large number of ADA cases. Plaintiffs typically lose those cases, even before Democratic appointees. The large number of ADA cases in our sample might make more recent appointees "look" conservative even if their overall voting patterns are not.

To respond to this problem, we examined the relative ideology of each president's appointees for each of the case types (table 6-1). To the extent that increasing conservatism in our data is an artifact of having more or less of particular case types for particular years, those effects should be cancelled by examining one case type at a time. The disclaimer here is that each case type represents a smaller sample size than the data set as a whole. As a result, some of the percentages should be taken with many grains of salt; in particular, the evident anomalies—for example, a 100 percent rate of liberal votes from nominees of President George W. Bush in some areas—are a product of a very small number of votes. Nonetheless, the overall pattern is at least suggestive.

The most general point is that if the appointees of Reagan, Bush I, and Bush II are aggregated *by particular area*, quite conservative voting patterns emerge—more conservative than those of the appointees of Eisenhower, Nixon, and Ford, taken together. Consider, for example, the area of affirmative action, which shows a 22 percent lower liberal voting rate from Reagan, Bush I, and Bush II appointees than from appointees of the three Republican predecessors, and the area of abortion, which shows a 17 percent lower liberal voting rate. By contrast, the Clinton appointees do not show much more conservative voting patterns, in particular areas, than those of Carter, Johnson, and Kennedy, taken as a whole. But controlling for area, it does seem that there has been an overall conservative trend within the federal courts of appeals, if only because of the more conservative voting patterns of appointees of recent Republican presidents (see table 6-2).

But this appearance, too, should not be taken as decisive. Even within case types, issues do not remain constant over time. It is possible, for example, that sex discrimination cases between 1990 and 1995 were quite different, and stronger for plaintiffs, than sex discrimination cases between 1996 and 2000. Even if judicial behavior is investigated within the same area of law, temporal changes in the nature of cases may mean that we lack a controlled experiment.

We have been emphasizing changing mixes of cases over time— a problem that much complicates efforts to "rank" presidents in terms of their judicial appointees. And as we have also noted, the case mix changes for another reason as well: Litigants respond to changes in the composition of the courts. This is not an artifact of our data; rather, it is a characteristic of the judicial system. Suppose that the judiciary were quite liberal in 1980 and moderately conservative by 1990. It should be expected that in the latter period, the calculus for those deciding whether to litigate would be quite different for plaintiffs and defendants alike. If, for example, a plaintiff is challenging an affirmative action program, his chances of success would be much greater in 1990 than in 1980 For that reason, the same such program is more likely to be challenged in the later period. At the same time, actual and potential defendants should be aware of the shifting composition of the judiciary. It follows that some affirmative action programs, in

Table 6-2. *Percentage of Liberal Votes by President Group and Case Category*[a]

Percent

| | Kennedy/ Johnson/ Carter | Clinton | Eisenhower/ Nixon/ Ford | Reagan/ Bush I | Bush II |
|---|---|---|---|---|---|
| All Cases | 55 (4,073) | 48 (3,580) | 48 (2,223) | 38 (8,883) | 38 (198) |
| Affirmative action | 75 (160) | 76 (46) | 62 (86) | 40 (189) | |
| Abortion | 63 (156) | 79 (38) | 62 (98) | 45 (140) | 0 (3) |
| Americans with Disabilities Act | 44 (410) | 42 (564) | 31 (164) | 26 (1,076) | 33 (39) |
| Campaign finance | 42 (52) | 47 (30) | 36 (25) | 28 (83) | 40 (5) |
| Capital punishment | 46 (112) | 43 (136) | 13 (30) | 22 (341) | 0 (5) |
| Contracts | 37 (70) | 11 (18) | 29 (49) | 22 (95) | 100 (1) |
| Criminal appeals | 37 (585) | 34 (965) | 34 (367) | 31 (2,207) | |
| Environmental Protection Agency | 60 (166) | 62 (87) | 65 (37) | 49 (249) | 75 (4) |
| Federalism | 95 (188) | 99 (219) | 96 (80) | 94 (456) | 94 (17) |
| Piercing corporate veil | 48 (65) | 32 (79) | 28 (32) | 25 (169) | |
| Sex discrimination | 55 (582) | 51 (669) | 42 (269) | 34 (1,686) | 32 (37) |
| Takings | 79 (223) | 92 (37) | 78 (117) | 76 (274) | 100 (3) |

*(continued)*

place in 1980, will be abolished on advice of counsel by 1990, simply because they are so vulnerable to legal challenge. It also follows that defendants, having lost in district court, will not appeal cases in 1990 that they would have appealed in 1980—and also that they will be likely to settle cases that they would have litigated in the earlier period.

Table 6-2. *Percentage of Liberal Votes by President Group and Case Category* (continued)
Percent

| | Kennedy/ Johnson/ Carter | Clinton | Eisenhower/ Nixon/ Ford | Reagan/ Bush I | Bush II |
|---|---|---|---|---|---|
| Title 7 | 43 (191) | 42 (223) | 38 (79) | 34 (582) | 14 (14) |
| Punitive damages | 66 (47) | 79 (62) | 65 (17) | 75 (134) | 75 (4) |
| First amendment | 56 (104) | 71 (24) | 64 (56) | 48 (103) | 33 (3) |
| Obscenity | 33 (186) | 33 (3) | 28 (241) | 25 (53) | 0 (1) |
| Gay and lesbian rights | 40 (15) | 88 (8) | 10 (10) | 19 (32) | |
| National Environmental Policy Act | 51 (47) | 40 (98) | 27 (15) | 19 (95) | 17 (18) |
| Desegregation | 77 (336) | 0 (0) | 64 (398) | 40 (5) | |
| Standing | 54 (195) | 38 110 | 0 7 | 44 450 | |
| Federal Communications Commission | 55 (71) | 65 (52) | 33 (6) | 52 (198) | |
| 11th amendment abrogation | 56 (66) | 63 (72) | 63 (27) | 34 (151) | 0 (2) |
| National Labor Relations Board | 52 (46) | 63 (40) | 31 (13) | 37 (115) | 100 (2) |

a. Number of votes in parentheses. Blank cells indicate no data available.

To attempt to control for this factor, we examined judicial votes, by president, over specified slices of time. Table 6-3 shows the results.[4] Compared to what we have shown thus far, this figure more plausibly suggests the degree of differences among recent presidents. A key claim—that Republican appointees are growing increasingly conservative—does have some support. The

Table 6-3. *Percentage of Liberal Votes by Presidential Group over Time*
Percent

| Liberal votes | 1981–84 | 1985–88 | 1989–92 | 1993–96 | 1997–2000 | 2001–04 |
|---|---|---|---|---|---|---|
| Kennedy/Johnson/ Carter | 52 (272) | 68 (210) | 60 (285) | 54 (716) | 53 (1,347) | 48 (753) |
| Clinton | | | | 53 (399) | 50 (1,404) | 45 (1,777) |
| All Democratic | 52 (272) | 68 (210) | 60 (285) | 54 (1,115) | 52 (2,751) | 46 (2,530) |
| Eisenhower/Nixon/ Ford | 49 (145) | 57 57(87) | 51 (82) | 45 (333) | 44 (552) | 37 (358) |
| Reagan/Bush I | 52 (46) | 49 (182) | 45 (359) | 43 (1,795) | 38 (3,752) | 33 (2,749) |
| Bush II | | | | | | 38 (198) |
| All Republican | 50 (191) | 52 (269) | 46 (441) | 43 (2,128) | 38 (4,304) | 34 (3,305) |
| Democrats differ from Republicans? | no | p < .01 | p < .05 | p < .01 | p < .001 | p < .05 |
| Differences among Democrats? | | | | no | no | no |
| Differences among Republicans? | no | no | no | no | p < .05 | no |
| More conservative than previous time period? | | No | p < .05 | no | p < .001 | no |

a. Number of votes in parentheses. Blank cells indicate no data available.

most striking evidence can be found between 1997 and 2000: Eisenhower/Nixon/Ford judges voted liberal 44 percent of the time, while Reagan/Bush I judges did so only 38 percent of the time. Overall, for the full 1981–2004 time period (and controlling for case category and circuit), Reagan/Bush I judges produced significantly more conservative votes than Eisenhower/Nixon/Ford judges ($p < .01$), a pattern that, if anything, is even stronger ($p < .001$) for the most recent half of the period 1993–2004. Note, too, that there is a smaller difference between Clinton appointees and those of previous Democratic appointees: In the same time period, Kennedy/Johnson/Carter judges voted 53 percent liberal, and Clinton appointees voted 50 percent liberal, a difference that is not significant.[5]

Also of interest—and a complication for assessing presidential appointees as such—is the *apparently increasing conservatism of each group of individual appointees over time.* Combining across all Republican appointees, there is a statistically significant trend over time toward more conservative voting, both for the full period 1981–2004 ($p < .001$) and also separately for the most recent half of the period 1993–2004 ($p < .001$).[6] For Democratic appointees, we have a similar tale: There is a statistically significant ($p < .01$) trend toward conservatism among Democratic appointees during the most recent half of the period 1993–2004, when Clinton judges entered the fray ($p < .001$), but no trend among Kennedy/Johnson/Carter judges in the earlier period.

Thus, for example, Reagan appointees appear significantly more conservative in 1993–1996 than they do in 1985–1988. Moreover, no group becomes more liberal after 1989–1992. Thus, Reagan/ Bush I judges from 1985–1988 cast liberal votes 49 percent of the time; from 1993–1996 they cast liberal votes 43 percent of the time; from 1997–2000, they cast liberal votes 38 percent of the time; and from 2001–2004, they were only 33 percent liberal. This is an unmistakably clear pattern, and similar ones are apparent for the other groupings. Hence we might be agnostic on whether one set of appointees is more liberal or conservative than another, but conclude that federal judges are becoming more conservative across time.

But there is a problem with this judgment as well. As we have noted, the case mix is not constant, and hence a decline in the percentage of liberal votes might reflect not increasing conservatism but increasing encounters with cases in which liberal votes are comparatively infrequent. Recall, for example, that the ADA was enacted in 1990 and that plaintiffs typically lose under this statute. To the extent that different cases are being litigated, it is difficult to reach confident conclusions about how to rank presidents in terms of the voting patterns of their appointees. We have attempted to minimize this influence in our findings by statistically controlling for case categories and also, in the analysis of table 6-3, by looking at relatively short, temporally adjacent periods. It seems very likely that some degree of conservative trend is indeed occurring.

Despite the large amount of data and our controls, we are unable to offer entirely confident rankings of various presidents in terms of the ideology of their judicial appointees. Taken as a whole, the data are consistent with the view that the most conservative appointees come from Ronald Reagan, George H. W. Bush, and George W. Bush, and that there are no substantial differences among the three presidents in terms of the ideological orientation of their appointees. But the difficulty of controlling for all confounding variables means that any conclusion to this effect must be taken with several grains of salt.

## Differences over Time

It would also be extremely valuable to have a sense of whether federal courts are becoming more conservative or more liberal over time. Our data suggest some plausible conclusions. There is a significant difference between Republican and Democratic appointees, and as the relative proportion changes, the ideological orientation of the federal courts will change as well. In 1970, for example, 59 percent of the federal judiciary had been appointed by a Democratic president. In 1980 that percentage was 57 percent. In 1990 the percentage was 33 percent. In 2000 it was 43 percent—and at the end of 2004 it was 37 percent. It would be reasonable to predict that, taken together, both party effects and panel effects would ensure increasing conservatism between 1980 and 2004—with increasing liberalism between 1992 and 2000. The role of panel effects deserves particular emphasis. Because of ideological dampening and ideological amplification, a greater percentage of Democratic or Republican appointees will have a larger effect than the raw numbers suggest.

It is possible, however, that an emphasis on party and panel will fail to capture the nature or extent of the change. As we have seen, some Republican presidents will appoint more conservative judges than others; and Clinton appointees are widely thought to be more conservative than Carter and Johnson appointees. In addition, some other variable might affect the nature and extent of the shift. Perhaps the Supreme Court, even without significant changes in its composition, is giving a clear signal that lower courts should move in one or another direction. Perhaps the Supreme Court has made it clear that in particular areas—for example, abortion, affirmative action, federalism, and campaign finance regulation—more conservative voting patterns are required. Indeed, Supreme Court guidance, often in conservative directions, has marked many of the areas that we have investigated.

Alternatively, some cultural shift may be reflected in judicial behavior. Judicial votes often seem to be affected by cultural changes, and perhaps some such changes contribute to the patterns that we observe. A reasonable conclusion seems to be that the federal courts are becoming more conservative. As before, however, this conclusion does not fully come to terms with an important confounding variable: the changing mix of cases. Consider in this light how odd it would be to test the ideological tendency of Supreme Court justices by asking about the total percentage of liberal votes in 2000, and by comparing that to the total percentage of such votes in 1980. It would not be terribly surprising if the overall percentage of liberal votes were the same in the two years. That result would not mean that the Court's ideological tendencies were unchanged; it merely would mean that a different mix of cases had come before the Court. It is because of the changing mix that any Supreme Court, whatever its composition, is likely to show a significant number of 5–4 splits. Litigants will ensure that the cases that reach the Court are difficult and that they will divide the justices. Something similar underlies the mix of cases in the courts of appeals.

We can, however, construct an analysis that partially addresses this concern by examining consecutive four-year periods. In this relatively brief time, changes in case mix are less likely to confound the analysis. To test the possibility of growing conservatism more precisely, we again ran logistic regressions using a dummy variable for time period to predict voting. These regressions also controlled for case category and circuit, and compared only the adjacent four-year periods defined in table 6-3 above. We find that there was no statistically significant difference in the rate of liberal voting between three of the five adjacent periods, but that there were highly significant shifts toward conservative voting between the other two (see bottom row of table 6-3). While it is a bit of a blunt instrument, this simple sequential analysis does show a slight overall trend toward conservatism over the last 25 years, even when controlling for case mix and the meaning of case categories.

## A General Note on Rational Litigants

We have emphasized that selection effects make it difficult to test various claims about ideological changes over time. Litigants adjust to shifting judicial ideology, and hence shifts in voting patterns may not occur even though judicial ideology has changed dramatically. A simple, crude hypothesis would be that because rational litigants will adjust their prospects to the possibility of success, the "litigation market" will ensure a 50 percent success rate in general and in many areas of the law. In fact, the overall level of success, in the cases we examine, is not so far from the baseline: Republican appointees offer liberal votes 40 percent of the time, and Democratic appointees do so 52 percent of the time.

Note, however, that the crude hypothesis might have to be adjusted if either plaintiffs or defendants are able to litigate more cheaply than the other side, or if the expected set of costs and benefits will distort the calculation of either side. If one side is subsidized by the taxpayers or by charity, the economic incentive may not impose its ordinary deterrent, and people will bring suits even if they are most unlikely to win. Or perhaps some litigants, in some areas, seek publicity rather than a victory; a highly publicized loss (by, say, an environmental group) might count as a net victory. And in criminal cases, defendants often do not have to pay for their appeals. Because liberty is at stake, it might be expected that those convicted of crime will challenge their convictions even if the likelihood of a successful appeal is well under 50 percent. The basic point is that whatever the exact percentages, litigants will unquestionably adjust to the changing composition of the federal judiciary.

How do these points bear on the conjecture that federal courts of appeals are becoming more conservative? If litigants are attentive to the mix of judges, then the overall rate of liberal votes should stay fairly constant over time. While Clinton appointees would be expected to show more liberal voting patterns than Reagan appointees, the overall level of liberal votes—in, say, 1988 and 1998—should not much vary. If rational litigants are adjusting their behavior to the ideological predispositions of the judiciary, the level of liberal votes ought not to change. Perhaps the hypothesis of rational litigation is unrealistic and too strict; perhaps litigation reflects certain forms of bounded rationality, or other biases, on the part of litigants. As we have suggested, there may well be a "lag time" before litigants adjust to the changes in the federal judiciary. But even if this is so, bounded rationality and "lag time" make it harder, not easier, to test any claim about ideological shifts over time.

To the extent that litigants do adjust, our findings might well understate the shift that we are exploring. Suppose that litigants adjust. If the percentage of liberal votes was still lower in 2004 than in 1988, notwithstanding adaptation by litigants, then there is good reason to believe that the federal judiciary is shifting significantly to the right—or, at the least, that it is shifting further to the right than litigants perceive. Unfortunately, however, the changing mix of case types makes it difficult to be confident about this judgment. It seems relatively clear that the ideological orientation of the federal judiciary will shift with a changing percentage of Democratic or Republican appointees; but beyond this, it is hazardous to draw inferences from the changing percentages of liberal votes over time.

## What about the Supreme Court?

In assessing movements within the lower federal courts, an additional complication, one to which we have referred only briefly, involves the role of the Supreme Court. Over the years we investigate, the Supreme Court has not remained constant in its composition or its instructions. Let us suppose, plausibly, that since 1980 the Supreme Court, under the leadership of Chief Justice William H. Rehnquist, was moving constitutional law in more conservative directions. If so, then we would expect to see a movement toward more conservatism from court of appeals judges, even if the ideological dispositions of those judges did not change at all. A shift toward more conservative voting would be purely an artifact of guidance from the Supreme Court. Indeed, the very same judicial personnel would shift, simply because of what the Supreme Court said. The question, then, is whether the changing pattern of votes reflects the influence of the Supreme Court or real differences in the ideological tendencies of presidential appointees.

On the basis of the data we have, it is possible to make some progress on this question. If the Supreme Court is moving the lower federal courts, then we should see the movement en masse. Democratic appointees in 1998 should show more conservative voting patterns than Democratic appointees in 1988—not because the former are more conservative, but because the former are dealing with more conservative rulings from the Supreme Court. Our data are consistent with this possibility; indeed, they provide some support for it. But movements from the Supreme Court cannot explain all of the shifts that we find. If the Supreme Court is responsible for the shift, then it should be expected that between 1985 and, say, 1988, there would be no difference between the votes of Nixon appointees and Reagan appointees; Nixon and Reagan appointees should show the same patterns, shifting in accordance with new guidance from the Supreme Court. Our evidence demonstrates, however, that even in the same time periods, recent Republican appointees show more conservative voting patterns than do less recent Republican appointees. Hence shifts on the Supreme Court cannot explain all of our findings.

## Inconclusive but Suggestive

Our goal in this chapter has been as much methodological as substantive. We have attempted to show exactly why it is so difficult to compare courts across either space or time. The most important factor involves the mix of cases: Because circuits decide different cases, because parties can choose whether to litigate, and because the federal docket in, say, 2004 was different from the federal docket in, say, 1990, a difference in the percentage of liberal votes tells us much less than we might at first believe.

Much of our analysis is therefore tentative. Nonetheless, we are confident about the following conclusions: As a circuit becomes more dominated by judges appointed by presidents of one political party, the circuit's voting patterns are highly likely to shift accordingly. If the federal courts have a growing percentage of Republican appointees, they are likely to become more conservative—not because every Republican appointee is conservative, or because every Democratic appointee is liberal, but because these are the general patterns we observe. Panel effects complement party effects, ensuring that every new appointee counts, in a sense, for more than one. Ideological dampening and ideological amplification are key factors here.

Our numerical comparisons, ranking courts of appeals and assessing changes across presidents and over time, should be taken with considerable caution. But—to end on an optimistic note—it is at least suggestive that those comparisons are consistent with the theoretical predictions just sketched.

# What Should Be Done?

## Of Politics, Judging, and Diversity

7

W e have found that in many areas, there is a significant difference between the voting patterns of Republican appointees and those of Democratic appointees. We also have found that on unified panels, ideological tendencies are amplified—and that the tendencies of isolated appointees are dampened. A key result is that panels consisting of three Republican appointees show systematically different outcomes than panels consisting of three Democratic appointees. To a substantial degree, the ideological tendencies of courts of appeals are correlated with the percentages of appointees by Republican and Democratic presidents. And within the courts, ideological shifts over time have a great deal to do with the same percentages. None of this denies the disciplining effects of law. In some areas, ideological differences are nonexistent. In most areas, they are not huge. But the presence of party and panel effects is undeniable.

These findings raise a host of questions. The United States has long been in the midst of an intense debate about the role of judicial "ideology" and "activism," both in general and in relation to the process of appointing and confirming federal judges. As we have emphasized, some of our findings offer a real testimonial to the constraints laid down by the rule of law. But we have also found that it is hopelessly inadequate to say that judges simply "follow the law." Often there is no law to follow; judges must exercise discretion. Much of the time, judicial convictions matter. Is this troubling? Is it bothersome to find a large effect from party or from panel composition? Should we be concerned if like-minded judges produce relatively extreme voting patterns? More generally: Is there reason to attempt to ensure diversity on the federal courts, or to promote a degree of diversity on panels? How, if at all, should political officials and citizens react to our findings?

When Republican appointees and Democratic appointees differ, it is often because their own commitments lead them to read the law in different ways—and sometimes in radically different ways. Many people seem to think that judges appointed by presidents of different political parties are not fundamentally different and that, once on the bench, judges frequently surprise those who nominated them. The view is not entirely baseless, but it is badly misleading. Some appointees do disappoint the presidents who nominated them, but those examples are far from typical. On the contrary, they are extremely rare, certainly at the level of the Supreme Court, where presidents usually end up getting what they wanted.[1] The same is broadly true in the lower courts, at least in the last decades. As we have seen, judges appointed by Republican presidents are systematically different, in their voting behavior, from judges appointed by Democratic presidents. This is true for the most contested issues of the day—affirmative action, sex

discrimination, abortion, capital punishment, environmental protection, disability discrimination, and much more. Most of the
time, Presidents Kennedy, Johnson, Nixon, Ford, Carter, Reagan,
Bush, Clinton, and Bush could not possibly be disappointed by
the voting patterns of their appointees.

To understand these findings, it is necessary to say a few words
about legal reasoning. Suppose that existing law does not clearly
resolve the question of whether an affirmative action program, or
a restriction on commercial advertising, is constitutional. Even if
this is so, the law will impose many constraints on what judges
can do. As the law now stands, judges cannot, for example, rule
that affirmative action programs, or restrictions on commercial
advertising, are *always* unconstitutional; the Supreme Court has
simply forbidden those conclusions. In dealing with the hard
questions, many courts will reason by analogy.[2] They will ask
whether the law in question is analogous to those that have been
upheld or struck down.

But what does the process of reasoning by analogy entail? To
know whether one case is analogous to another, it is necessary to
make some kind of judgment about policy or principle. If one affirmative action plan is to be seen as "analogous" to another, it is
because the two plans share relevant similarities. A judgment about
relevant similarities requires the judge to identify, or to create, the
legally governing principle—one that unifies or separates the two
cases. If, for example, an affirmative action program is upheld
because it is not rigid, and because it allows officials to consider
many factors other than race, then the court is saying that affirma
tive action programs will be upheld so long as they are not rigid.[3]
That judgment might well depend on an abstract judgment about
the best way to understand the idea of equality ("equal protection") under the Constitution.

The prominent legal theorist Ronald Dworkin, for example, argues that legal reasoning involves an effort to put previous decisions in the best constructive light, by identifying the best principle that accounts for them.[4] On an alternative view, legal reasoning might depend on a more pragmatic judgment—one that depends on an assessment of the consequences of one or another approach. Richard Posner, for example, contends that an assessment of policy, and of consequences, underlies the exercise of analogical reasoning.[5]

Of course, many cases do not involve that form of reasoning at all. Often the court is asked to interpret an ambiguous statute, such as the Clean Air Act, the Federal Communications Act, or the National Labor Relations Act. When the law leaves gaps or uncertainties, ideological convictions appear to matter. Perhaps they matter because judges try to make the best possible sense out of ambiguous statutes, and Democratic and Republican appointees differ about the best way to do that. Perhaps convictions matter because consequences matter, and different judges evaluate consequences in different ways. Perhaps different judges bring different "background presumptions" to the law, and those different background presumptions are correlated with the political party of the appointing president.

Let us put the complexities to one side. Whatever the best account of legal reasoning, it should be unsurprising to find that Republican and Democratic appointees differ in ideologically charged cases. As a statistical regularity, the two sets of appointees will make different judgments about both policy and principle. If they are searching for analogies, their searches will not produce the same results, because what seems analogous to one person will not so seem to another. Some people might find a ban on commercial advertising to be similar to a ban on political dissent; other people might find the two to be entirely different. In general, the presence of different judgments, operating across party lines, is no embarrassment to the law. Different judgments are a predictable product of a system of law that contains gaps and uncertainties. They are a tribute to the inevitable fact that when judges are exercising the creativity to which analogical reasoning or statutory interpretation entitles them, they will differ.

We have emphasized that, across party lines, the relevant differences are large but not massive. Because of the disciplining effect of precedent, and because judges do not radically disagree with one another, there is often significant commonality across the appointees of presidents of different parties. But in the most difficult areas—those where the law is unclear or in flux—both party and panel effects are large enough to matter a great deal both to the particular litigants and to the development of the law. Moreover, the difficult areas are the ones that matter most.

## Who's Right?

It might seem hard to know how to respond to our findings without taking a stand on the merits—without knowing what we want judges to do. Suppose that three Republican appointees are especially likely to strike down affirmative action programs and that three Democratic appointees are especially likely to uphold those programs. Suppose that three Republican appointees are likely to rule against people complaining of disability discrimination and that three Democratic appointees are far more likely to rule in their favor. At first glance, one or the other inclination is troubling only if we know whether we disapprove of one or another set of results. Maybe the Republican appointees are correct. If so, the

Democratic appointees are causing all the trouble. If Republican appointees are less inclined to rule in favor of disabled people, or women complaining of sex discrimination, they might be right, simply because they are reading the law properly.

The appropriate response, as some Republican voters and politicians believe, is to ensure that the federal courts are dominated by Republican appointees, who will move the law in the right directions. Or the right response, as some Democratic voters and politicians believe, may be to populate the courts with more Democratic appointees, so as to ensure better outcomes. Suppose, then, that a view about what judges should do is the only possible basis for evaluation. If so, we might conclude that those who prefer judges of a particular party should seek judges of that party—and that group influences are essentially beside the point. The best approach is to go issue by issue and to see which set of judges is more likely to be right, and to argue long and hard on behalf of those judges and their stands. If Democratic or Republican appointees are usually right, the lesson of our findings is the importance of obtaining judges of the right kind, and of persuading those who err of their errors.

The effort to move the Supreme Court in one or another direction is best understood in this light. Some people believe that the Court has severely blundered by, for example, ruling in "liberal" directions too often in the last decades. Others believe that the Court has not been "liberal" enough, indeed that it has been too conservative, and that it should be pushed to the left—especially because a more liberal Supreme Court should be expected to lead the lower courts in more liberal directions as well. The same debate can be found in the less visible disagreements over the future of the lower federal courts.

## Diversity?

But it is much too simple, we think, to read our findings as (only) a reason to seek judges of the preferred sort. Begin with a simple point: In some cases, the law, properly interpreted, does point toward one or another conclusion. Ideological tendencies, whatever they are, can be distorting. In general, the existence of diversity on a three-judge panel is likely to bring the law to light and perhaps to move the panel's decision in the direction of what the law requires. The existence of diverse judges and a potential dissent increases the probability that the law will be followed. And even where the law is unclear, it is valuable to have competing views about how it should be understood.

Suppose that the law does not clearly say whether a woman, complaining of sex discrimination, should be permitted to submit her case to a jury. There are real benefits in ensuring that competing arguments are made within a three-judge panel. Recall here that unified panels show much more political voting patterns in reviewing the decisions of the NLRB, the EPA, and the FCC. It is not exactly wonderful if all-Republican panels show a strong preference for the decisions of Republican administrations, and if all-Democratic panels show a strong preference for the decisions of Democratic administrations.

Of course, Republican appointees do not always agree with one another, and of course, there is disagreement among Democratic appointees as well. The difference among Republican appointees can be greater than the difference between any particular Republican and Democrat. But we have nonetheless encountered major divergences in voting patterns along party lines. At least if it is not entirely clear who is right, in general or in particular cases, a degree of diversity is desirable. To be sure, a Democratic president cannot appoint people who have been appointed by a Republican president. But we think that it is desirable to have different sorts of judges on the bench, and any particular president, and any particular Senate, would do well to keep this point in mind.

The *Chevron* study, referred to in chapter 4, strongly supports this point.[6] The presence of a potential dissenter—in the form of a judge appointed by a president from another political party—creates a possible whistleblower, who can reduce the likelihood of an incorrect or lawless decision.[7] The same lesson emerges from the highly politicized behavior, just described, of unified panels reviewing the decisions of the NLRB, the EPA, and the FCC. Through an appreciation of the nature of group influences, we can see the wisdom in an old idea: *A decision is more likely to be right, and less likely to be political in a bad sense, if it is supported by judges with different predilections.*

There is a further point. Suppose that in many areas, it is not clear in advance whether the appointees of Democratic or Republican presidents are correct. Suppose that we are genuinely uncertain, at least to some degree. If so, then there is reason to favor a situation in which the legal system has diverse judges, simply on the ground that through that route, more reasonable opinions are likely to be heard. If we are uncertain, then there is reason to favor a mix of views merely by virtue of its moderating effect. In the face of uncertainty, many people choose between the poles, and sensibly so.[8]

Does it seem odd to want diverse views on a court of appeals? Consider an analogy. A significant amount of modern law is made by independent regulatory commissions, such as the Federal Trade Commission, the Securities and Exchange Commission, the National Labor Relations Board, and the Federal Communications Commission. Some of the time, such agencies act through adjudication. They resolve disputes about the meaning of the legal terms; they function in essentially the same fashion as federal courts. Here is the key point: Under federal statutes, Congress has ensured, through explicit legal mandate, that these agencies are not monopolized by either Democratic appointees or Republican appointees. The law requires that no more than a bare majority of the agency's leaders may be from a single party.[9] Why is this?

An understanding of group influences, and of the risk of ideological amplification, helps to justify this important requirement. A regulatory agency whose leaders are all-Democratic or all-Republican might move toward an extreme position—indeed, toward a position that is more extreme than that of the median Democrat or Republican, and possibly more extreme than that of any agency official standing alone. A requirement of bipartisan membership can operate as a check against extreme movements of this kind. Some members of Congress may well have been intuitively aware of this general point. At the very least, it can be said that Congress was closely attuned to the policymaking functions of the relevant institutions, and it was careful to provide a safeguard against extreme movements.

Why does the United States fail to create similar safeguards for courts? Part of the answer must lie in a firm belief that, unlike heads of independent regulatory commissions, judges are not policymakers. Their duty is to follow the law, not to make policy. An attempt to ensure bipartisan composition would seem inconsistent with a commitment to this belief; it might even compromise the view, widely and properly held, that the law has real priority in the judicial enterprise. For this reason, a serious proposal for bipartisan composition of federal judicial panels would predictably produce a degree of outrage and caricature. Few people are arguing for a system in which all courts must have mixed panels, that is, panels with both Democratic and Republican appointees. But the evidence we have discussed shows that judges are policymakers of an important kind—and that in some contexts, their political commitments very much influence their votes. In principle, there is good reason to attempt to ensure a mix of perspectives within courts of appeals.

We are not prepared to suggest a formal requirement that federal tribunals should be balanced along party lines; such a requirement would raise many complexities. But in the abstract, a mix is much better than uniformity. Nor is the general idea entirely out of keeping with actual practice. Those who lose before three-judge panels are permitted to ask for "en banc" review, that is, review by the full circuit (or sometimes by a large segment of it). In en banc review, it is inevitable that both Republican and Democratic appointees will be hearing the case. And because en banc review typically involves some of the most difficult and controversial cases, the system already includes a mechanism for ensuring diverse perspectives, at least some of the time. A real virtue of en banc review is that it operates as a safeguard against those situations in which unified panels produce extreme outcomes, simply by virtue of their unity.

Of course, the idea of diversity, or of a mix of perspectives, is hardly self-defining. It would not make sense to say that the federal judiciary should include people who refuse to obey the Constitution, or who will let the president do whatever he wants, or who think that the Constitution allows suppression of political dissent or does not forbid racial segregation. Here, as elsewhere, no one really wants diversity as such; the domain of appropriate diversity is limited. What is necessary is reasonable diversity, or diversity of reasonable views, and not diversity in the abstract. People can certainly disagree about what reasonable diversity entails in this context. All that we are suggesting here is that there is such a thing as reasonable diversity—and that it is important to ensure that judges, no less than anyone else, are exposed to it, and not merely through the arguments of advocates.

## A Counterargument

A competing argument would stress a possible purpose or at least a function of the lower federal courts: to produce a wide range of positions so that Supreme Court review will ultimately follow an exploration of a number of possible interpretations. For those who emphasize the value of diverse decisions, what we have treated as a vice might instead be a virtue. In an important essay, Heather Gerken has emphasized the value of "second-order diversity"—of ensuring diversity not *within* institutions, but *across* institutions, so that different groups offer different perspectives to the public at large.[10] The federal system, for example, benefits from second-order diversity. There are differences in the policies and initiatives of California, Texas, Michigan, North Carolina, Georgia, Massachusetts, Utah, and New York, and the nation as a whole can learn a great deal from seeing the effects of those policies and initiatives. So, too, with educational institutions: If some universities have distinctive positions, and form specified "schools," knowledge can benefit as a result—even if the diversity operates system-wide rather than within every particular institution. Gerken's central point is that sometimes diversity can be found system-wide simply *because* there is less diversity within the units and institutions that compose it. We might even seek system-wide diversity at the expense of diversity within particular units and institutions.

Perhaps the judiciary is not fundamentally different. On this view, it is desirable to have unified panels of ideologically similar judges, simply in order to produce a wide band of arguments for the Supreme Court to assess. One effect of the situation that we describe is that federal courts will generate a great range of positions and rationales. For affirmative action and campaign finance, for sex discrimination and environmental protection, the existence of all-Republican and all-Democratic panels will provide the Supreme Court, and the nation, with a great deal of information. All-Republican panels will reach outcomes, and will generate rationales, from which the Supreme Court should ultimately learn something; so, too, with all-Democratic panels. Perhaps that information, and the resulting variety, is worth a great deal.

We do not contend that this is an irrelevant concern; it does weigh in the balance. For the system as a whole, more (reasonable) positions are better than fewer. Second-order diversity can be exceedingly valuable for the legal system. We would respond only that Supreme Court review is exceedingly rare and that, most of the time, court of appeals decisions are effectively final. In these circumstances, it is not clear that the gain in the range of ideas outweighs the risks of error and unequal treatment. In particular, it is a serious problem if the fate of a lawsuit, large or small, turns on the random assignment of judges to the particular panel. Similarly situated people will be treated differently, and for no good reason.

In any case, diverse views, on any particular panel, are likely to be helpful. A three-judge panel may produce outcomes, and arguments, that are different and better if they include a mix of perspectives. The whistleblower point is particularly important here. If three-judge panels sometimes do as they do because of the absence of a whistleblower, the resulting diversity is nothing to celebrate. Recall that unified Republican panels are more favorable to environmental, communications, and labor decisions under Republican leadership than under Democratic leadership—and that unified Democratic panels favor such decisions under Democratic leadership. Surely this is a major problem in a system that is committed to impartial justice.

## The Senate

We think that our findings cast fresh light on one of the most sharply disputed issues of our time: the legitimate role of the Senate in giving "advice and consent" to presidential appointments to the federal judiciary. When the president nominates someone to the Supreme Court, or to a lower federal court, what should the Senate consider?

Some people firmly believe that the Senate should restrict itself to the qualifications, character, and competence of a nominee—that it should not concern itself with ideology or "judicial philosophy." On this view, the Senate does not legitimately consider the likely voting patterns of a nominee; whether a nominee is "liberal" or "conservative" or something else is quite beside the point. Others insist that it is appropriate for Republican senators to contest Democratic nominees whose views seem to them unacceptable, and so, too, for Democratic senators contesting Republican nominees. Some version of the latter view has clearly prevailed. In 2005 many Democrats objected to the nomination of Justice Samuel Alito, largely on the ground that his views were too extreme; in the same year, many Republicans objected to the nomination of Ms. Harriet Miers, partly on the ground that she was not a reliable conservative. It is now agreed, by all sides, that some views are legitimately taken as disqualifying. If a nominee believes that the Constitution permits racial segregation, or does not protect free speech, or forbids the president from acting as commander in chief of the armed forces, she cannot be confirmed. The real contest is over what falls in the category of unacceptable views.

Empirical findings cannot resolve that contest. But an understanding of the evidence outlined here can easily be taken to support the view that the Senate has a responsibility to exercise its constitutional authority in order to ensure a reasonable diversity of views. The original understanding of the Constitution strongly supports an independent role for the Senate in consenting to the appointment of federal judges—a role in which the likely pattern of judicial votes is a relevant consideration.[11] In the founding understanding, the Senate was supposed to act as a check on the president's choices, and the check included an inquiry into the nominee's anticipated judgments and predispositions. The nation's long history, as it has developed over time, supports that independent role as well.[12] Because of its independent role in the system of checks and balances, the Senate is certainly entitled to consider the general approach of potential judges on the federal bench.

There can be no doubt that the president considers the general approach of his nominees. Democratic presidents do not want to appoint extreme conservatives or judges with certain positions; Republican presidents do not want to appoint extreme liberals or judges with certain predilections. The Senate is at least entitled to consider a nominee's general approach as well. Under good conditions, these simultaneous powers should bring about a healthy form of mutual constraint, permitting each branch to counter the other. Indeed, that system can be seen as part and parcel of social deliberation about the direction of the federal judiciary. Thus far, then, the analysis suggests that the constitutional plan is best read as calling for a significant role for the Senate as well as the president, creating a system that ought to lead in the direction of diversity. And as part of that plan, the Senate is entitled to monitor the president's choices so as to ensure that the federal judiciary has the appropriate mix of views.

Why might this view be rejected? It could be urged that there is only one legitimate approach to constitutional or statutory interpretation—that, for example, some version of "originalism" or "textualism," now supported by some conservatives, is the only such approach, and that anyone who rejects that view is unreasonable. On this view, it might be said that the Constitution must be understood to mean what it meant at the time that it was ratified[13]—and any other view should be ruled off-limits, even if that other view would produce "diversity." Or it could be urged that *Roe v. Wade* was rightly decided and that any judge who rejects *Roe*, or the right of privacy, is unacceptable for that reason alone. Some liberals appear to believe that, at least for the Supreme Court, approval of *Roe v. Wade* is a precondition for a favorable vote from the Senate. For true believers, it is pointless to argue for diverse views.[14] Diversity is not necessary or even valuable if we already know what should be done and if competing views would simply cloud the issue. In a scientific dispute, it is not helpful to include those who believe that the earth is flat.

Alternatively, it might be urged that, even in light of our findings, the Senate should defer to the president's judgments, aside from investigating issues of competence and character. Here is the key point: A deferential role for the Senate, combined with natural political competition and ordinary cycles within the electorate, might well produce a sensible mix of views over time. Republican senators should defer to Democratic presidents, and Democratic senators should defer to Republican presidents, in a way that will ensure sufficient diversity. Of course, the nation elects presidents of both parties. It is possible that the right kind of diversity can be achieved even if the Senate takes a highly deferential role toward presidential choices. On this view, the only problem is practical: How to obtain an agreement by which Democratic senators defer to Republican presidents in return for deference by Republican senators to Democratic presidents.

In any case, it is not unreasonable to suppose that when a president is chosen, it is because the public supports his general approach to most issues, including those that reach the federal judiciary. If a particular president's judicial appointees move in one direction, we may be witnessing a form of democracy in action. If the federal judiciary moved to the right under President George W. Bush, it was because the democratic process was working as it should. We have seen likely rightward movement under Presidents Ronald Reagan, George H. W. Bush, and George W. Bush; and perhaps this is what the nation (or at least a majority) wanted. Under our system, moreover, one-party domination is not likely to occur for lengthy periods—and if anything like it does occur, it is because the public is in favor of the party that is dominating. Perhaps the Senate can restrict itself to a passive role and can assume that the appropriate level of diversity will emerge as a result of changes in the party affiliation of the president.

We do not deny this possibility. Nor have we dismissed the suggestion that unified panels have some real advantages. Our only suggestions are that reasonable diversity on the federal judiciary is desirable, that the Senate is entitled to pursue such diversity, and that without diversity, there is a risk of unequal treatment and a danger that judicial panels will go in extreme and unjustified directions. In the long run, it may well be worth considering more ambitious proposals, designed not to strengthen the role of the Senate but to ensure both quality and an appropriate mix of views over time. An obvious possibility would be for presidents to rely on a bipartisan commission, one that would produce a range of names, including people who are noteworthy both for their distinction and (taken as a group) their range of views. Perhaps such a commission could attempt to ensure appropriate diversity within the courts.

Under the Constitution, of course, presidents could not be bound by the recommendations of any commission. But perhaps presidents could voluntarily take account of the resulting recommendations. Doubtless many variations could be imagined on this theme.

## The Future

The proper approach to the Constitution and to federal law has raised some of the most heated debates of the last fifty years (and more). No empirical findings can resolve that debate. But it is possible to identify the areas in which Republican and Democratic appointees disagree most sharply, and it is also possible to show where their views are most entrenched. It is certainly noteworthy that on federal courts of appeals the two sets of judges do not disagree on criminal appeals and in cases involving punitive damages, property rights, standing to sue, and congressional power under the Commerce Clause. It is also noteworthy to find sharp differences in cases involving affirmative action, the National Environmental Policy Act, sex discrimination, and gay and lesbian rights. With an understanding of where judges most differ, national debate can be more informed about the competing tendencies. At the very least, we can show that it is inadequate to say that appellate judges simply "follow the law." We can also show that the ideological differences are significant but not overwhelming—that the rule of law imposes its discipline even on the most contested issues.

We have made a tentative plea in favor of ideological diversity, on the theory that such diversity is a valuable way of checking extremism and of exposing competing views. Ideological amplification is not always wrong. Perhaps the most extreme view is best. But there is reason to have more confidence that decisions are right, and that justice has been done, if diverse judges have been able to agree with one another.

# Conclusion

## Law and Politics:
## A Mixed Verdict

No reasonable person seriously doubts that ideology, understood as moral and political commitments of various sorts, helps to explain judicial votes. Presidents are entirely aware of this point, and their appointment decisions are undertaken with full appreciation of it. Senators are aware of this point as well, and throughout American history, they have sometimes checked presidential choices for that reason. Of course, judges adhere to the law, but where the law is not plain, judicial convictions play an inevitable role.

We have found striking evidence of a relationship between the political party of the appointing president and judicial voting patterns. For the most important questions, Republican appointees differ from Democratic appointees. Hence we see significant differences in such areas as campaign finance legislation, disability discrimination, affirmative action, sex discrimination, environmental protection, labor law, and much more. In these and other domains, differences between Republican and Democratic appointees are a simple fact of life in a way that significantly affects the outcomes of lawsuits and the lives of ordinary Americans.

We have also found that, much of the time, judicial votes are affected by panel composition, producing both ideological dampening and ideological amplification. Begin with dampening: In many domains, the voting patterns of isolated Democratic appointees, sitting with two Republican appointees, look like the overall voting patterns of Republican appointees—just as the voting patterns of isolated Republican appointees are akin to the overall voting patterns of Democratic appointees. Ideological amplification is pervasive as well. In many domains, a Democratic appointee is significantly more likely to vote in the stereotypical liberal fashion if surrounded by two Democratic appointees than if surrounded by one Republican and one Democrat. Similarly, the voting patterns of Republican appointees are very much influenced by having two, rather than one, judicial colleagues appointed by a president of the same political party; in such cases, Republican appointees show notably conservative voting patterns.

Taken as a whole, the data suggest the pervasiveness of four phenomena. The first is ideological voting: significant splits between Republican and Democratic appointees on the great legal issues of the day. The second is the collegial concurrence: a vote to join two colleagues and to refuse to dissent publicly, notwithstanding a possible disposition to vote the other way and perhaps a continuing belief that the decision is incorrect. The third is group polarization: the tendency of a group of like-minded people, including judges, to move to relative extremes. The fourth is a whistleblower effect, by which a single judge of a different party from the court's majority can have a moderating effect on a judicial panel. We are willing to speculate that our findings, focused as they are on votes rather than opinions, understate the effect of ideological amplification. The opinions of all-Republican and all-Democratic panels are likely to be quite extreme. We are also willing to speculate that the essential patterns that we describe can be found in many domains of social life; some of them may well be pervasive or near-universal features of human interaction.

It might be surprising to find that in some controversial areas, the political affiliation of the appointing president is *not* correlated with judicial votes, and hence that in those areas, none of these effects can be observed. This is the basic finding for criminal appeals, takings of property rights, punitive damages, standing to sue, and Commerce Clause challenges to national legislation. But it should not be terribly shocking to see that, in the areas of abortion and capital punishment, party matters but panel composition does not. In these areas, judges vote their convictions, and they are unaffected by the views of the other judges on the panel. What is perhaps most striking is that in our data set, abortion and capital punishment are the only areas in which party effects are unaccompanied by panel effects. (Recall that in the context of gay and lesbian rights, the sample size is too small to permit a judgment about panel effects.)

These findings cannot resolve the most intense debates about the future of the federal judiciary. By itself, empirical evidence will not dictate conclusions about how panels should be composed or about what federal judges ought to do. But if divided panels increase the likelihood of effective whistleblowing, and if unified panels tend to go to extremes, there may well be good reason to attempt to ensure a high degree of intellectual diversity within the federal courts. Of course, this claim would not hold if the appointees of one or another party had a monopoly on legal wisdom. In most areas, however, we think that there is no such monopoly and that better results are likely to come from a mix of views and inclinations.

We have also explored differences across circuits and across time. It is possible to make a provisional "ranking" of circuits in ideological terms. We have seen that when the Supreme Court issues a major decision, Republican and Democratic appointees tend to agree for a period—but that differences expand over time as the meaning of the decision becomes disputed in the context of novel and sometimes unanticipated debates. Finally, there is some reason to believe that the federal courts have been moving to the right—and that the appointees of Presidents Reagan, George H. W. Bush, and George W. Bush have essentially the same ideological tendencies.

However the most difficult issues are resolved, the principal empirical findings are clear. In many domains, Republican appointees vote very differently from Democratic appointees, and ideological tendencies are both dampened and amplified by the composition of the panel.

## APPENDIX
### Logistic Regression Results
Dependent variable = liberal vote

| Predictor | Coefficient | SE | z | P > \|z\| |
|---|---|---|---|---|
| Party (Republican = 0, Democrat = 1) | .63 | .04 | 16.17 | .00 |
| Other panel members (number of Democrats) | .33 | .03 | 11.69 | .00 |
| Affirmative action | 1.39 | .18 | 7.85 | .00 |
| Abortion | 1.38 | .18 | 7.64 | .00 |
| Americans with Disabilities Act | .29 | .16 | 1.86 | .06 |
| Campaign finance | .42 | .22 | 1.95 | .05 |
| Capital punishment | .24 | .18 | 1.39 | .17 |
| Environmental Protection Agency | 1.25 | .18 | 6.99 | .00 |
| Piercing corporate veil | .17 | .19 | .88 | .38 |
| Sex discrimination | .75 | .15 | 4.88 | .00 |
| Title 7 | .59 | .16 | 3.60 | .00 |
| First Amendment | 1.19 | .19 | 6.14 | .00 |
| Obscenity | .14 | .18 | .80 | .42 |
| Gay and lesbian rights | .11 | .32 | .36 | .72 |
| National Environmental Policy Act | .01 | .20 | .03 | .98 |
| Desegregation | 1.88 | .17 | 11.10 | .00 |
| Federal Communications Commission | 1.40 | .20 | 7.07 | .00 |
| 11th Amendment abrogation | .89 | .19 | 4.70 | .00 |
| National Labor Relations Board | .93 | .21 | 4.39 | .00 |
| 1st Circuit | .22 | .10 | 2.24 | .03 |
| 2nd Circuit | .33 | .09 | 3.72 | .00 |
| 3rd Circuit | .78 | .11 | 7.39 | .00 |
| 4th Circuit | .07 | .10 | .74 | .46 |
| 5th Circuit | .03 | .08 | .41 | .68 |
| 6th Circuit | .09 | .09 | 1.05 | .30 |
| 8th Circuit | .08 | .08 | 1.00 | .32 |
| 9th Circuit | .53 | .09 | 6.16 | .00 |
| 10th Circuit | .26 | .09 | 2.76 | .01 |
| 11th Circuit | .22 | .09 | 2.29 | .02 |
| D.C. Circuit | .02 | .10 | .19 | .85 |
| Constant | −1.78 | .16 | −11.08 | .00 |

*(continued)*

151

## Logistic Regression Results (continued)
Dependent variable = liberal vote

*Summary statistic*
Base case = 7th Circuit, contracts cases, Republican
Log likelihood    −7845.5

| | |
|---|---|
| N | 12,417 |
| $\chi^2$ (30) | 1255.3 |
| Prob > $\chi^2$ | .0000 |
| Pseudo $R^2$ | .074 |

# Notes

## Chapter One

1. There are many good discussions of judicial behavior, based on other kinds of data sets; we shall refer to some of these discussions below. For a general sampling, see Frank B. Cross, "Decisionmaking in the U.S. Courts of Appeals," 91 *Cal. L. Rev.* 1457 (2003); Nancy Scherer, *Scoring Points: Politicians, Political Activists and the Lower Federal Court Appointment Process* (Stanford University Press, 2004); Lee Epstein and Jeffrey A. Segal, *Advise and Consent: The Politics of Judicial Appointments* (Oxford University Press, 2005).

2. *See* Cross, *supra* note 1, at 1514 (reporting empirical finding that law strongly disciplines judicial judgments).

3. *See* Jeffrey A. Segal and Harold J. Spaeth, *The Supreme Court and the Attitudinal Model Revisited* (Oxford University Press, 2002). For an important study of politics and lower courts, see Scherer, *supra* note 1.

4. For valuable historical background, see Scherer, *supra* note 1. The use of party of appointing president as a proxy for judicial ideology has come under attack for its imprecision. *See* Lee Epstein and Gary King, "Empirical Research and the Goals of Legal Scholarship: The Rules of Inference," 69 *U. Chi. L. Rev.* 1 (2002). One possible alternative relies on "common space" scores. These were originally developed to measure the ideology of legislative and executive actors. *See* Keith T. Poole and Howard Rosenthal, *Congress: A Political-Economic History of Roll Call*

*Voting* (Oxford University Press, 1997) (common space scores for Congress); Nolan M. McCarty and Keith T. Poole, "Veto Power and Legislation: An Empirical Analysis of Executive and Legislative Bargaining from 1961 to 1986," 11 *J. L. Econ. & Org.* 282 (1995) (same for presidents). The common space score is determined by collecting a representative's votes on many issues and placing them along a single ideological dimension. Several studies have subsequently used the common space score of the judge's home state senator, the appointing president, or some combination thereof. *See, e.g.,* Michael Giles, Virginia A. Hettinger, and Todd Peppers, "Picking Federal Judges: A Note on Policy and Partisan Selection Agendas," 54 *Pol. Res. Q.* 623 (2001) (using the mean common space score of a judge's home state congressional delegation); Susan W. Johnson and Donald R. Songer, "The Influence of Presidential Versus Home State Senatorial Preference on the Policy Output of Judges on United States District Courts," 36 *L. & Soc'y Rev.* 657 (2002) (comparing the use of senatorial to presidential common space scores); Gregory C. Sisk and Michael Heise, "Judges and Ideology: Public and Academic Debates about Statistical Measures," 99 *Nw. U. L. Rev.* 743 (2005) (discussing methodological debates in the literature and using common space scores to code for ideology in a study of voting in religious cases); Jennifer L. Peresie, "Female Judges Matter: Gender and Collegial Decisionmaking in the Federal Appellate Courts," 114 *Yale L. J.* 1759 (2005) (using common space scores in a study of gender influences on voting in Title VII cases). Note that, as with our party of the appointing president variable, the common space score measures the ideology of an actor involved in the judge's appointment, rather than measuring the ideology of the particular judge.

5. *See id.*

6. 410 U.S. 113 (1973).

7. In fact, sophisticated efforts have been made to study judicial ideology itself and to use it to predict and to analyze votes in particular areas. For a valuable example, with citations to the relevant literature, see Peresie, *supra* note 4. Our focus, as noted in the text, is on the political affiliation of the appointing president; we emphasize that this is not the same as judicial ideology. In fact, the party of the appointing president is rightly criticized as a crude proxy for ideology.

8. *See* Roger Brown, *Social Psychology: The Second Edition* (New York: Free Press, 1985).

9. For accounts of aggregate data, see Cross, *supra* note 1, at 1504–09 (showing significant effect of ideology, varying across administrations).

10. Codified at 42 U.S.C. § 4321 et seq. (2005).

11. *See also* Cross, *supra* note 1, at 1504–05 (describing similar findings based on aggregate data). For a valuable study of peer influences within the judiciary in affirmative action cases, see Charles M. Cameron and Craig P. Cummings, "Diversity and Judicial Decision-Making: Evidence from Affirmative Action Cases in the Federal Courts of Appeals, 1971–1999" (2003) (unpublished manuscript), available at www.yale.edu/coic/CameronCummings.pdf. [February 5, 2006].

12. For an overview of conformity pressures, see Solomon E. Asch, "Opinions and Social Pressure," in *Readings about the Social Animal* (Elliot Aronson ed.) (New York: W. H. Freeman 1984).

13. *See* Brown, *supra* note 8; David Schkade, Cass R. Sunstein, and Daniel Kahneman, "Deliberating about Dollars: The Severity Shift," 100 *Colum. L. Rev.* 1139, 1140 (2000); *see also* Cameron and Cummings, *supra* note 11, at 19–21 (finding a similar effect in affirmative action cases, where liberal judges become far less inclined to support affirmative action programs when surrounded by conservatives and conservative judges become far more approving when surrounded by liberals).

14. *See* Frank B. Cross and Emerson H. Tiller, "Judicial Partisanship and Obedience to Legal Doctrine: Whistleblowing on the Federal Courts of Appeals," 107 *Yale L. J.* 2155 (1998).

15. *See* Asch, *supra* note 12.

16. *See* Robert Baron and Norbert Kerr, *Group Process, Group Decision, Group Action,* 2nd ed. (Open University Press, 2003).

17. *See* Brown, *supra* note 8, at 203–26.

18. *See* Segal and Spaeth, *supra* note 3.

19. *See id.* at 86. We oversimplify a complex account.

20. Note that the disciplining effect of existing law will be most constraining in disputes that never find their way to litigation; in many such cases, everyone agrees what the law is, and it is not worthwhile to test that question. In disputes that are not litigated, it is safe to say that Republican appointees and Democratic appointees would agree almost all of the time. The doctrine should be expected to impose less discipline in cases that go to trial. In addition, the decision to appeal suggests a degree of indeterminacy in the law. Hence we are considering cases that are not only contested ideologically but that also involve a sufficient lack of clarity in the law to make it worthwhile to challenge a lower court ruling. Of course, the highest degree of indeterminacy can be found in cases that are litigated to the Supreme Court. In the areas in which we find no effects from ideology—criminal appeals, takings,

punitive damages, FCC, federalism, and standing to sue—such effects may nonetheless be found at the Supreme Court level. In fact, we predict, with some confidence, that they would.

21. For a valuable discussion, see Cross, *supra* note 1, which involves aggregate data and does not explore particularly controversial areas, and thus provides a useful supplement to ours. The effect of judicial ideology is usefully investigated in Linda R. Cohen and Matthew L. Spitzer, "Solving the *Chevron* Puzzle," 57 *Law & Contemp. Probs.* 65 (Spring 1994) (special issue) (finding that a justice is far more likely to defer to an agency's statutory construction when the agency is controlled by a president of the same political party as the justice). There is an informative, but sparse, literature on panel effects. *See* Burton M. Atkins, "Judicial Behavior and Tendencies towards Conformity in a Three Member Small Group: A Case Study of Dissent Behavior on the U.S. Court of Appeals," 54 *Soc. Sci. Q.* 41 (1973); Burton M. Atkins and Justin J. Green, "Consensus on the United States Courts of Appeals: Illusion or Reality?" 20 *Am. J. Pol. Sci.* 735 (1976); Sheldon Goldman, "Conflict and Consensus in the United States Courts of Appeals," 1968 *Wis. L. Rev.* 461; Donald R. Songer, "Consensual and Nonconsensual Decisions in Unanimous Opinions of the United States Courts of Appeals," 26 *Am. J. Pol. Sci.* 225 (1982). We have found especially valuable Cross and Tiller, *supra* note 14, and Richard L. Revesz, "Environmental Regulation, Ideology, and the D.C. Circuit," 83 *Va. L. Rev.* 1717 (1997). On partisan voting, see Revesz, *supra*. A helpful overview of party effects is Daniel R. Pinello, "Linking Party to Judicial Ideology in American Courts: A Meta-analysis," 20 *Just. Sys. J.* 219 (1999).

## Chapter Two

1. With regard to search criteria, we tried to choose the method that would achieve the largest number of results. Once we performed the searches as listed, we further filtered the body of cases so as to ensure that the data set would be limited to relevant cases. For example, in the capital punishment context, when we searched for "capital punishment" on Lexis, we found relevant cases as well as irrelevant ones. Irrelevant cases would include, for instance, a non-capital punishment case citing a capital punishment case. *See, e.g.*, Hines v. United States, 282 F.3d 1002, 1004 (8th Cir. 2002) (citing a capital punishment case and including the words "capital punishment" in citation even though *Hines* was a non-

capital punishment case). In the affirmative action context, some irrelevant cases noted (inconveniently, for us) that "Congress has not taken an affirmative action." Since these cases did not bear on what we were studying, they were not included in the final search results.

2. We assembled the sample of abortion cases by searching Lexis for "core-terms (abortion) and date aft 1960 and constitutional" and "abortion and constitution!" These cases generally presented challenges to statutes and policies that might infringe on a woman's right to choose, or challenges to the constitutionality of anti-protesting injunctions. (We included the latter set of cases both because they are plausibly seen as "abortion cases" and because their inclusion increases the size of a fairly small sample. It would be possible to object that these cases are properly treated as "free speech cases" rather than "abortion cases," but we hypothesized that the abortion issue would inevitably be salient, a hypothesis that is supported by our findings about judicial voting patterns.) Because plaintiffs differed among the cases, outcomes were coded as pro-life or pro-choice; if a judge voted at all to support the pro-life position, then the vote was counted as a pro-life vote. A case that is typical of the sample is *Planned Parenthood* v. *Casey*, 947 F.2d 682 (3rd Cir. 1991) (finding various provisions of Pennsylvania's Abortion Control Act constitutional, but finding the spousal notice provision unconstitutional). The sample includes cases from January 1, 1971, through June 30, 2004. We identified a total of 146 cases.

3. We assembled the sample of capital punishment cases by searching Lexis for "capital punishment" (a search term that may have resulted in a few omissions, but not many). If a judge voted to grant the defendant any relief, then the vote was coded as a pro-defendant vote. A case that is typical of the sample is *Hampton* v. *Page*, 103 F.3d 1338 (7th Cir. 1997) (rejecting inmate's request for writ of habeas corpus in death penalty case). The sample includes cases from January 1, 1995, through June 30, 2004. We identified a total of 208 cases.

4. 42 U.S.C. §§ 12101 et seq. (2005). We assembled the sample of disability cases by searching Lexis for "Americans with Disabilities Act." If a judge voted to grant the plaintiff any relief, then the vote was coded as a pro-plaintiff vote. A case that is typical of the sample is *Mack* v. *Great Dane Trailers*, 308 F.3d 776 (7th Cir. 2002) (ruling against employer on ADA claim). The sample includes cases from January 1, 1998, through June 30, 2004. We identified a total of 751 cases.

5. We assembled the sample of criminal cases from the D.C. Circuit, the Third Circuit, and the Fourth Circuit by searching

www.ll.georgetown.edu/federal/judicial/cadc.cfm, http://vls.law.vill.edu/
Locator/3/, and www.law.emory.edu/4circuit/2nd-idx.html for cases with
"United States" in the title. Government appeals and civil disputes were
disregarded. If a judge voted to grant the defendant any relief, then the
vote was coded as a pro-defendant vote. A case that is typical of the sample is *United States* v. *Mason*, 233 F.3d 619 (D.C. Cir. 2000) (reversing
conviction where district court erred as a matter of law in not instructing the jury on defendant's innocent possession defense). The sample
includes cases from January 1, 1995, through June 30, 2004. We identified a total of 1,387 cases.

6. We assembled the sample of takings cases by shepardizing on Lexis
*Lucas* v. *South Carolina Coastal Council*, 505 U.S. 1003 (1992); *Nollan*
v. *California Coastal Commission*, 483 U.S. 825 (1987); *Keystone Bitu-
minous Coal Ass'n* v. *DeBenedictis*, 480 U.S. 470 (1987); and *Penn Central Transportation Co.* v. *New York City*, 438 U.S. 104 (1978). If a
judge voted to grant the party alleging a violation of the Takings Clause
any relief, then the vote was coded as a pro-plaintiff vote. A case that is
typical of the sample is *Eastern Enters.* v. *Chater*, 110 F.3d 150 (1st Cir.
1997) (ruling that the Coal Act did not violate the Takings Clause). The
sample includes cases from June 26, 1978, through June 30, 2004. We
identified a total of 220 cases. We did not include decisions of the U.S.
Court of Federal Claims.

7. We assembled the sample of Contracts Clause cases by shepardizing on Lexis *Allied Structural Steel Co.* v. *Spannaus*, 438 U.S. 234 (1978)
and *United States Trust Co. of New York* v. *New Jersey*, 431 U.S. 1
(1977). If a judge voted to grant the party alleging a violation of the
Contracts Clause any relief, then the vote was coded as a pro-plaintiff
vote. A case that is typical of the sample is *Baltimore Teachers Union* v.
*Mayor of Baltimore*, 6 F.3d 1012 (4th Cir. 1993) (holding city plan
reducing employee salaries by one percent permissible under the Contracts Clause). The sample includes cases from April 27, 1977, through
June 30, 2004. We identified a total of 78 cases.

8. We assembled the sample of affirmative action cases by searching
Lexis for "affirmative action and constitution or constitutional." The
sample also includes cases found through a Westlaw Key Cite of *United
Steelworkers of America, AFL-CIO-CLC* v. *Weber*, 443 U.S. 193 (1979)
and *Regents of University of California* v. *Bakke*, 438 U.S. 265 (1978).
If a judge voted to hold any part of an affirmative action plan unconstitutional, then the vote was considered a vote for the party challenging
the plan. A case that is typical of the sample is *International Brotherhood*

*of Electrical Workers v. Hartford*, 625 F.2d 416 (2d Cir. 1980) (upholding affirmative action program's constitutionality). The sample includes cases from June 28, 1978, through June 30, 2004. We identified a total of 161 cases.

9. We assembled the sample of Title VII cases by searching Lexis for "Title VII and African-American or black." We included cases that presented a challenge by an African-American plaintiff. If a judge voted to grant the plaintiff any relief, then the vote was coded as a pro-plaintiff vote. A case that is typical of the sample is *Grant v. News Group*, 55 F.3d 1 (1st Cir. 1995) (ruling against plaintiff in Title VII civil rights action). The sample includes cases from January 1, 1985, through June 30, 2004. We identified a total of 363 cases.

10. We assembled the sample of sex discrimination cases by searching Lexis for "sex! discrimination or sex! harassment." Some of the cases included retaliation claims. If the plaintiff was afforded any relief, then the vote was coded as a pro-plaintiff vote. A case that is typical of the sample is *Hartsell v. Duplex Prods.*, 123 F.3d 766 (4th Cir. 1997) (finding against employee in sexual harassment case brought under Title VII). The sample includes cases from January 1, 1995, through January 30, 2004. We identified a total of 1,081 cases.

11. We assembled the sample of campaign finance cases by shepardizing on Lexis *Buckley v. Valeo*, 424 U.S. 1 (1976). If a judge voted to afford the party challenging the campaign finance provision any relief, then the vote was coded as a pro-plaintiff vote. A case that is typical of the sample is *Carver v. Nixon*, 72 F.3d 633 (8th Cir. 1995) (finding Missouri's campaign contribution limit unconstitutional). The sample includes cases from January 30, 1976, through June 30, 2004. We identified a total of 65 cases.

12. We assembled the sample of sexual harassment cases (a subset of sex discrimination cases) by searching Lexis for "sex! harassment." Some of the cases included retaliation claims. If a judge voted to afford the plaintiff any relief, then the vote was coded as a pro-plaintiff vote. A case that is typical of the sample is *Hartsell*, 123 F.3d at 766 (finding against employee in sexual harassment case brought under Title VII). The sample includes cases from January 1, 1995, through June 30, 2004. We identified a total of 517 cases.

13. We assembled the sample of piercing-the-corporate-veil cases by searching Lexis for "pierc! and corporate veil." If a judge voted to afford the party trying to pierce the veil any relief, then the vote was coded as a liberal vote. A case that is typical of the sample is *Marzano v. Computer*

*Science Corp.*, 91 F.3d 497 (3d Cir. 1996) (refusing to pierce the corporate veil in context of employment discrimination lawsuit). The sample includes cases from January 1, 1995, through June 30, 2004. We identified a total of 116 cases.

14. We relied on Jay E. Austin et al., *Judging NEPA: A "Hard Look" at Judicial Decision Making Under the National Environmental Policy Act*, available at www.endangeredlaws.org/downloads/JudgingNEPA. pdf, for our sample of NEPA cases. We excluded from analysis unpublished opinions and those heard in the Federal Circuit. A case that is typical of the sample is *Sierra Club* v. *United States Army Corps of Eng'rs*, 295 F.3d 1209 (11th Cir. 2002) (rejecting environmental organization's claim that the Army Corps of Engineers had failed to consider the impact of a planned toll road on various species). The sample includes 91 cases from January 1, 2001, through January 20, 2005.

15. We assembled the sample of gay and lesbian rights cases by searching Westlaw and Lexis for "homosexual" and "gay rights." These cases generally presented challenges to statutes and policies that might infringe on gay and lesbian rights or discrimination claims by gay and lesbian plaintiffs. A case that is typical of the sample is *Padula* v. *Webster*, 822 F.2d 97 (D.C. Cir. 1987) (holding that FBI hiring decision did not infringe upon applicant's right to equal protection, and that the FBI's specialized functions rationally justified consideration of gay and lesbian conduct). The sample includes 22 cases from January 1, 1980, through January 30, 2004.

16. We assembled the sample of Eleventh Amendment cases by shepardizing on Lexis *Seminole Tribe* v. *Florida*, 517 U.S. 44 (1996). These cases generally asked whether Congress had properly abrogated the states' Eleventh Amendment immunity under a statute such as the Americans with Disabilities Act, 42 U.S.C. §§ 12101 et seq. (2005), or the Family Medical Leave Act, 29 U.S.C.S. § 2601 (2005). If a judge voted to hold that Congress had properly abrogated state sovereign immunity, then the vote was coded as a "liberal" vote. If a judge voted to hold that Congress had not validly abrogated state sovereign immunity, then the vote was coded as a "conservative" vote. A case that is typical of the sample is *Anderson* v. *State Univ. of New York*, 169 F.3d 117 (2nd Cir. 1999) (finding that the Equal Pay Act validly abrogates the states' Eleventh Amendment immunity from suit in federal court). The sample includes cases from February 16, 1996, through April 6, 2005. We identified a total of 106 cases.

17. We assembled the sample of commercial speech cases by shepardizing on Lexis *Virginia State Bd. of Pharmacy* v. *Virginia Citizens Consumer*

*Council*, 425 U.S. 748 (1976), and *Central Hudson Gas & Electric Corp.*
v. *Public Service Comm'n*, 447 U.S. 557 (1980). These cases generally presented challenges to federal and state statutes, city ordinances, or federal
and state agency orders and regulations that restricted commercial speech,
most often in the form of commercial advertising or solicitation. The decisions typically weighed the government's interest in the regulation against
the speaker's First Amendment rights. If a judge voted to strike down a regulation as unconstitutional, then the vote was coded as "unconstitutional." A case that is typical of the sample is *Anheuser-Busch* v. *Schmoke*,
63 F.3d 1305 (4th Cir. 1995) (holding city ordinance banning billboard
advertising of alcoholic beverages constitutional). The sample includes
97 cases from March 30, 1978, through February 14, 2004.

    18. We assembled the sample of punitive damage cases by searching
Lexis for "punitive damages." These cases presented constitutional or
statutory challenges to punitive damage awards. If a judge voted to
affirm the award of punitive damages, then the vote was coded as a "vote
to affirm." A case that is typical of the sample is *Inter Med. Supplies,
Ltd.* v. *Ebi Med. Sys.*, 181 F.3d 446 (3d Cir. 1999) (remitting jury's
award of punitive damages) (Garth dissenting). The sample includes
88 cases from September 12, 1996, through December 19, 2003.

    19. We assembled the sample of obscenity cases by shepardizing on
Lexis *Miller* v. *California*, 413 U.S. 15 (1973), *Roth v. United States*, 354
U.S. 476 (1957), and *A Book Named "John Cleland's Memoirs of a
Woman of Pleasure"* v. *Attorney General of Massachusetts*, 383 U.S. 413
(1966). If a judge voted to grant the defendant any relief, including holding the material in question not in violation of the obscenity law or finding the obscenity statute or ordinance unconstitutional, then the vote
was coded as a pro-defendant vote. Cases that are typical of the sample
are *Walker* v. *Dillard*, 523 F.2d 3 (4th Cir. 1975) (finding statute limiting
obscenity to be overbroad and therefore unconstitutional) and *United
States* v. *Slepicoff*, 524 F.2d 1244 (5th Cir. 1975) (affirming defendant's
convictions for mailing obscene material). The sample includes 178 cases
from January 1, 1957, through March 1, 2005.

    20. We assembled the sample of EPA cases by shepardizing *Chevron
U.S.A. Inc.* v. *Natural Res. Def. Council, Inc.*, 467 U.S. 837 (1984), and
searching for challenges to EPA decisions. A vote counted as liberal if it
favored upholding an agency's decision that was against industry attack,
or if it favored striking down an agency's decision in the face of a challenge by a public interest group. These proxies for ideology were treated
only as presumptive; in a very few cases, an investigation of the context

produced different assessments. A case that is typical of the sample is *Louisiana Envtl. Action Network* v. *EPA*, 172 F.3d 65 (D.C. Cir. 1999) (denying public interest challenge to EPA rulemaking). The sample includes 181 cases from June 25, 1984, through August 1, 2005.

21. We assembled the sample of FCC cases by shepardizing *Chevron*, 467 U.S. at 837, and searching for challenges to FCC decisions. A vote counted as liberal if it favored upholding an agency's decision that was against industry attack, or if it favored striking down an agency's decision in the face of a challenge by a public interest group. These proxies for ideology were treated only as presumptive; in a very few cases, an investigation of the context produced different assessments. A case that is typical of the sample is *Cellco Partnership* v. *FCC*, 357 F.3d 88 (D.C. Cir. 2004) (denying industry petition for review of FCC action). The sample includes 109 cases from June 25, 1984, through August 1, 2005.

22. We assembled the sample of NLRB cases by shepardizing *Chevron*, 467 U.S. at 837, and searching for challenges to NLRB decisions. A vote counted as liberal if it favored upholding an agency's decision that was against industry attack, or if it favored striking down an agency's decision in the face of a challenge by a public interest group. These proxies for ideology were treated only as presumptive; in a very few cases, an investigation of the context produced different assessments. A case that is typical of the sample is *ITT Indus., Inc.* v. *NLRB*, 413 F.3d 64 (D.C. Cir. 2005) (denying petition for review). The sample includes 72 cases from June 25, 1984, through August 1, 2005.

23. We assembled by searching Lexis for "segregation" and by shepardizing *Plessy* v. *Ferguson*, 163 U.S. 537 (1896), *Brown* v. *Bd. of Educ.*, 347 U.S. 483 (1954), and *Missouri ex rel. Gaines* v. *Canada*, 305 U.S. 537 (1938) during four time periods: 1905–55, 1956–65, 1966–75, and 1976–85. The sample includes school desegregation cases, and racial segregation cases more generally, from 1945–85. The votes were generally coded as pro–school board (or other defendant) or pro-plaintiff. A pro-plaintiff vote was considered a liberal vote. A case that is typical of the sample is *Bradley* v. *School Board of Richmond*, 317 F.2d 429 (4th Cir. 1963) (plaintiff students entitled to injunction against continuation of school's discriminatory practices). We identified a total of 314 cases.

24. We assembled the sample of D.C. Circuit standing cases by searching Lexis for "standing" and "injury in fact." A vote to grant a party standing was coded as a liberal vote. A case that is typical of the sample is *National Federation of Federal Employees* v. *United States*, 905 F.2d 400

(D.C. Cir. 1990) (finding that union had standing to raise constitutional claims against United States and Department of Defense). The sample includes 254 cases from January 1, 1990, through January 13, 2004.

25. We assembled the sample of Commerce Clause cases by shepardizing *United States* v. *Lopez*, 514 U.S. 549 (1995). If a judge voted to afford the plaintiff any relief, then the vote was coded as a pro-plaintiff vote. A case that is typical of the sample is *United States* v. *Bramble*, 103 F.3d 1475 (9th Cir. 1996) (upholding various statutes under the Commerce Clause). The sample includes cases from April 26, 1995, through June 30, 2004. We identified a total of 320 cases.

26. Thus we extended the viewscreen to earlier cases when the post-1995 sample was small. In deciding how far back to look, we typically relied on starting dates marked by important Supreme Court decisions that predictably would be cited in relevant cases.

27. For simplicity of analysis and clarity of presentation, we coded votes for all case types in the same ideological direction. Identical results would come using conservative votes but with the sign reversed.

28. In the same vein, see Cross, *supra* note 1, chapter 1, at 1504–05.

29. Here, we exempt cases in which there is little or no ideological voting. If those cases were included, then we would see the same overall patterns, but in diminished form. If we exempt cases of ideological voting without panel effects (abortion, capital punishment), the aggregate panel effects would, of course, be more pronounced.

30. The data were analyzed using a logistic regression model with the *vote* (liberal/conservative) of an individual judge in a given case as the dependent variable. The independent variables were the judge's *party* (Democratic/Republican appointee), the number of Democratic appointees among the other two judges on the *panel*, and dummy variables for *case category* and *circuit*. Results for this overall model appear in the Appendix. For analyses of individual case categories, the model is the same but with *case category* dummies dropped; for analyses of circuits, the *circuit* dummies are dropped. In the aggregate analysis of figure 1, the coefficients for party ($p < .001$) and panel ($p < .001$) are both highly significant.

31. The coefficients for party ($p < .001$) and panel ($p < .001$) are both highly significant.

32. 42 U.S.C. § 4332(C) (2005).

33. *See* Austin et al., *supra* note 14.

34. The coefficients for party ($p < .001$) and panel ($p < .001$) are both highly significant.

35. The coefficients for party ($p < .001$) and panel ($p < .05$) are both significant.

36. The coefficients for party ($p < .001$) and panel ($p < .01$) are both highly significant.

37. The coefficients for party ($p < .001$) and panel ($p < .001$) are both highly significant.

38. The sample is already very large here, so we thought it unnecessary to collect earlier data to test our three hypotheses.

39. The coefficients for party ($p < .001$) and panel ($p < .001$) are both highly significant.

40. Our findings should be compared with those of another study, which found that a judge's gender does matter in the context of sexual harassment cases in federal courts of appeals. *See* Peresie, *supra* note 4, chapter 1 (studying cases from 1999–2001).

41. The coefficient for party is significant ($p < .05$), and the coefficient for panel is in the right direction but of marginal significance ($p = .09$). We include campaign finance cases in this group of case categories because it has a similar overall pattern.

42. The coefficients for party ($p < .05$) and panel ($p < .05$) are both significant.

43. *See* Revesz, *supra* note 21, at 1721–27.

44. The coefficients for party ($p < .05$) and panel ($p < .01$) are both significant.

45. Using a smaller data set than that used here, Dean Revesz finds that when industry challenges an environmental regulation, there is an extraordinary difference between the behavior of a Republican majority and that of a Democratic majority. Republican majorities reverse agencies over 50 percent of the time; Democratic majorities do so less than 15 percent of the time. Revesz, *supra* note 21, chapter 2, at 1763; Richard L. Revesz, "Ideology, Collegiality, and the D.C. Circuit: A Reply to Chief Judge Harry T. Edwards," 85 *Va. L. Rev.* 805, 808 (1999).

46. *See* Revesz, *supra* note 21, chapter 2, at 1751–56; Revesz, *supra* note 45, at 808.

47. The coefficients for party ($p < .01$) and panel ($p < .05$) are both significant.

48. The coefficient for party is significant ($p < .05$), and the coefficient for panel is not. We include it here because it has a similar overall pattern.

49. 347 U.S. 483 (1954).

50. The coefficient for party is highly significant ($p < .01$), and the coefficient for panel is in the right direction but of marginal significance

($p$ = .08). We include segregation cases in this group of case categories because it has a similar overall pattern.

51. Neither the coefficient for party nor that for panel (both p < .20) achieves significance, but both are in the same direction as the other categories in this section.

52. Article I, § 10, cl. 1.

53. *See* Richard A. Epstein, "Toward a Revitalization of the Contract Clause," 51 *U. Chi. L. Rev.* 703, 704–05 (1984).

54. The coefficient for party is not significantly different from zero ($p$ > .30), but the panel coefficient is significant ($p$ < .05).

55. *Virginia State Bd. of Pharmacy* v. *Virginia Citizens Consumer Council*, 425 U.S. 748 (1976).

56. Neither the coefficient for party ($p$ = .13) or that for panel ($p$ = .07) achieves significance, but both are in the same direction as the other categories in this section.

57. These figures come from the multinomial probabilities of getting at least two votes to uphold (a *yes* vote, "Y"), given the panel composition. For a three-judge panel, there are four ways to uphold a decision— votes of YYY, YYN, YNY, and NYY, from judges *1*, *2*, and *3*, respectively. For example, for an all-Democratic–appointed panel ("DDD"), the probability of a judgment to uphold the program is P(YYY) + P(YYN) + P(YNY) + P(NYY) = .7*.7*.7 + .7*.7*(1-.7) + .7*(1-.7)*.7 + (1-.7)*.7*.7 = .343 + .147 + .147 + .147 = .784, which rounds to 78 percent; for one Republican and two Democrats ("RDD"), the calculation is .4*.7*.7 + .4*.7*(1-.7) + .4*(1-.7)*.7 + (1-.4)*.7*.7 = .196 + .084 + .084 + .294 = .658; and so forth.

58. If the shape of the graph were to hold up, it would suggest that the largest disparities occur when Democratic appointees are in the majority. This conclusion is tentative, of course, because of the lack of a clean or simple measure of the "true" party difference, since judges only vote on panels with other judges and never alone.

59. *See* Thomas Miles and Cass R. Sunstein, "Do Judges Make Regulatory Policy? An Empirical Investigation of *Chevron*," *U. Chi. L. Rev.* (forthcoming 2006).

## Chapter Three

1. The overall difference between Republican and Democratic appointees—a 31 percent vs. a 35 percent chance of a liberal vote—is of

little practical significance, but because of the extremely large number of criminal cases (over 1,300 cases and over 4,000 votes), the coefficient for party is statistically significant ($p < .01$). The coefficient for panel is not significant, despite the huge sample.

2. The coefficient for party is statistically significant ($p < .01$), but the difference between a 94 percent and a 97 percent chance of a liberal vote is of little practical significance. The coefficient for panel is not significant.

3. *See* Geoffrey R. Stone et al., *Constitutional Law* 200–210(5th ed., Aspen Law and Business, 2005).

4. *See* United States v. Morrison, 529 U.S. 598 (2000); United States v. Lopez, 514 U.S. 549 (1995).

5. U.S. Const. amend. V.

6. The coefficient for party is statistically significant ($p < .05$), but the difference between a 77 percent and an 80 percent chance of a liberal vote is of little practical significance. The coefficient for panel is not significant.

7. The informal lore receives support from Douglas T. Kendall and Charles P. Lord, "The Takings Project: A Critical Analysis and Assessment of the Progress So Far," 25 *B.C. Envtl. Aff. L. Rev.* 509 (1998).

8. For general discussion, see Cass R. Sunstein, David Schkade, Reid Hastie, John Payne, and W. Kip Viscusi, *Punitive Damages: How Juries Decide* (University of Chicago Press, 2002).

9. Neither the party nor the panel effect is statistically significant.

10. A key case was *Association of Data Processing Services Org. v. Camp*, 397 U.S. 150 (1970).

11. *See, e.g.*, Lujan v. Defenders of Wildlife, 504 U.S. 555 (1992).

12. Neither the party nor the panel coefficient is significant.

13. The coefficient for party is highly significant ($p < .001$), but the coefficient for panel is not.

14. The coefficient for party is highly significant ($p < .001$), but the coefficient for panel is not.

15. The coefficient for party is highly significant ($p < .001$), but the coefficient for panel is not.

## Chapter Four

1. Recall that many of the easiest cases are unpublished, but that a large number of easy cases in the criminal domain still find their way into publication.

2. *See* Nancy Scherer, "Are Clinton's Judges 'Old' Democrats or 'New' Democrats?" 84 *Judicature* 150, 154 (2000).

3. Along the same lines, see Cross, *supra* note 1, chapter 1.

4. See the discussion of how group influences are weakest in easy cases and when people have strong convictions, in Cass R. Sunstein, *Why Societies Need Dissent* (Harvard University Press, 2003).

5. Revesz, *supra* note 21, chapter 1, at 1764.

6. *See* the overview in Solomon E. Asch, "Opinions and Social Pressure," in *Readings About the Social Animal* 13 (Elliott Aronson ed.) (New York: W. H. Freeman, 1995).

7. *See* David Schkade, Reid Hastie, and Cass R. Sunstein, *What Happened On Deliberation Day?* (unpublished manuscript, University of Chicago, 2006); Richard S. Crutchfield, "Conformity and Character," 10 *Am. Psychologist* 191 (1955).

8. *See* Crutchfield, *supra* note 7.

9. *See* David Krech et al., *Individual in Society* 509 (New York: McGraw Hill, 1962).

10. *See* Asch, *supra* note 6.

11. *See* Asch, *supra* note 6.

12. Solomon Asch, *Social Psychology* 453 (Oxford: Oxford University Press, 1952).

13. Asch, *supra* note 6, at 13.

14. *Id.* at 16.

15. *Id.*

16. *See* Roger Brown, *Social Psychology: The Second Edition* 203–26 (New York: Free Press, 1985).

17. *See* David G. Myers, "Discussion-Induced Attitude Polarization," 28 *Hum. Rel.* 699, 707–12 (1975).

18. *See* Brown, *supra* note 16, at 224.

19. *See id.*

20. *See id.*

21. *See* David Schkade, Cass R. Sunstein, and Daniel Kahneman, *supra* note 13, chapter 1, at 1140–41.

22. *See* Reid Hastie, David Schkade, and Cass R. Sunstein, *What Happened on Deliberation Day?* (unpublished manuscript 2006).

23. *See* Brown, *supra* note 111, at 212–22; Sunstein, *Why Societies Need Dissent, supra* note 99, at 120–24; Robert S. Baron et al., "Social Corroboration and Opinion Extremity," 32 *J. Experimental Soc. Psychol.* 537 (1996).

24. *See* David Myers, *Intuition: Its Powers and Perils* 116–19 (Yale University Press, 2002).

25. *See* Brown, *supra* note 16, at 215–16; Sunstein, *supra* note 4, at 122–23.

26. *See* Baron et al., *supra* note 23, at 537–38.

27. *See* Mark Kelman et al., "Context-Dependence in Legal Decision Making," 25 *J. Legal Stud.* 287, 287–88 (1996).

28. *See* Baron et al., *supra* note 23, at 559.

29. *See* Sunstein, *supra* note 4.

30. *See* Baron and Kerr, *supra* note 16, chapter 1.

31. Insofar as the governing precedent was produced by another court of appeals, it might be a product of an all-Republican or an all-Democratic panel, producing a form of path dependency. Many complications are created by the possibility that an isolated judge would blow the whistle by asking a panel to conform to the beliefs of an earlier panel with a different and distinctive ideological composition. We are emphasizing here cases in which the precedent was produced by the Supreme Court, not a lower court.

32. *See* Cross and Tiller, *supra* note 14, chapter 1, at 2156.

33. 467 U.S. 837, 844 (1984).

34. *See* Cross and Tiller, *supra* note 14, chapter 1, at 2169.

35. Constructed on the basis of data in Cross and Tiller, *supra* note 14, chapter 1, at 2171–73.

36. *See id.* at 2174–76.

37. *See* Thomas Miles and Cass R. Sunstein, "Do Federal Judges Make Regulatory Policy? An Empirical Study," *U. Chi. L. Rev.* (forthcoming 2006).

## Chapter Five

1. *See* Scherer, *supra* note 1, chapter 1.

2. 347 U.S. 483 (1954).

3. 163 U.S. 537 (1896).

4. *See* Michael Klarman, *From Jim Crow to Civil Rights* (Oxford University Press, 2003).

5. This party difference approaches but does not achieve significance $p < .20$.

6. The small sample size limits our ability to find significant effects here.

7. 410 U.S. 113 (1973).

8. Neither the party nor panel effects are significant.

9. 354 U.S. 476 (1957).

10. 413 U.S. 15 (1973).

11. 354 U.S. at 484.

12. 413 U.S. at 24.

13. The party effect approaches significance ($p = .17$), but the panel effect is not significant.

14. Both the party ($p < .05$) and panel ($p < .05$) effects are highly significant.

15. *See* Scherer, *supra* note 1, chapter 1.

16. This possibility finds support in the literature. *See, e.g.,* Richard Fallon, Jr., "Legitimacy and the Constitution," 118 *Harv. L. Rev.* 1787, 1831–1832 (2005) (noting that, for at least a decade after the decision, *Brown* v. *Board of Education* met "massive resistance" through much of the South before sentiment hardened).

17. *See* Richard Kluger, *Simple Justice* (New York: Random House, 2004).

18. *See id.*

19. *Planned Parenthood* v. *Casey*, 505 U.S. 833 (1992).

20. *Id.*

21. *Id.*

## Chapter Six

1. We refer to the general courts of appeals; the more specialized Federal Circuit is typically categorized separately.

2. To provide a common basis for comparing the circuits, we analyzed those case types with party differences; we excluded punitive damages, federalism, takings, standing, and criminal appeals.

3. Of course, since our cases occurred over many years, an analysis that more carefully matched the year of the case with the then-current composition of the relevant circuit could show a stronger relationship.

4. For each time period, we ran a logistic regression identical to that for figure 2-1 in chapter 2, with individual votes as the dependent variable, and dummy variables for the president groupings, case type, circuit, and panel as the predictors. Thus, party in the original regression is replaced by dummy variables for the presidents.

5. The raw difference between Clinton and Kennedy/Johnson/Carter is statistically significant but becomes non-significant when we control for case category.

6. Again, these are from the same overall logistic regression, which controls for case category and circuit.

## Chapter Seven

1. *See* Epstein and Segal, *supra* note 1, chapter 1.

2. *See* Edward Levi, *An Introduction to Legal Reasoning* (University of Chicago Press, 1949); Cass R. Sunstein, *Legal Reasoning and Political Conflict* (Oxford University Press, 1996).

3. *See* Grutter v. Bollinger, 539 U.S. 306 (2003).

4. *See* Ronald Dworkin, *Law's Empire* (Harvard University Press, 1985).

5. *See* Richard A. Posner, *The Problems of Jurisprudence* (Harvard University Press, 1999).

6. *See* Cross and Tiller, *supra* note 14, chapter 1.

7. This is the explanation in *id.* at 2173.

8. *See* Mark Kelman et al., "Context-Dependence in Legal Decision Making," in *Behavioral Law and Economics* 61 (Cass R. Sunstein ed.) (Cambridge University Press, 2000).

9. *See, e.g.,* 15 U.S.C. § 78d(a) (2000) (stating that the SEC shall be composed of five commissioners appointed by the president, not more than three of whom shall be members of the same political party).

10. *See* Heather Gerken, "Second-Order Diversity," 118 *Harv. L. Rev.* 1099 (2005).

11. David A. Strauss and Cass R. Sunstein, "The Senate, the Constitution, and the Confirmation Process," 101 *Yale L. J.* 1491, 1494 (1992).

12. *See* Epstein and Segal, *supra* note 1, chapter 1.

13. *See* Antonin Scalia, *A Matter of Interpretation* (Princeton University Press, 1999).

14. Note, however, that even if it would be appropriate for all judges to share a certain approach, it is also desirable to have diversity with respect to the application of that approach. Textualists do not all agree with one another; there is internal diversity in the world of originalism. Diversity is appropriate here to ensure an airing of reasonable views.

# Index

appointing president and case category, 113, 114–15t, 116; voting pattern by presidential group and case category, 116–17, 118–19t; voting pattern by presidential group over time, 118–22, 120t, 128. *See also specific president by name*
Property rights cases. *See* Takings cases
Punitive damages, cases on, 11, 12, 49t, 52–53, 61, 145

Racial desegregation cases: aftermath of Supreme Court rulings on, 88, 89–91, 90f; ideological voting in, 26f, 36–37; *1945–65* period and panel effects, 89–90, 90f; *1966–75* period and panel effects, 90–91, 90f; *1976–85* period and panel effects, 90f, 91; prior to Supreme Court rulings on, 99; voting patterns over time in, 101–02, 103–04
Random assignment of judges and panel effects, 82–83
Rational litigants and effect on voting patterns over time, 125–26
Reagan, Ronald: judicial appointees of, 6, 7, 113, 116–17, 120–21, 122, 127, 144, 150; Supreme Court nominees of, 2. *See also* Presidents
Reciprocity, importance of, 66–67
Rehnquist, William H., 44
Republican appointees: differences from Democratic appointees, vii–viii, 5–7, 122–23, 129, 147. *See also* Conservative voting patterns; Party effects; *specific presidents*
Revesz, Richard, 34, 63
"Right" decisions, reaching of, 133–34. *See also* Whistleblower effect
Roberts, John, 2

*Roe v. Wade (1973)*, 6, 92, 143. *See also* Abortion cases
*Roth v. United States (1957)*, 93–94. *See also* Obscenity
Rule of law and judicial ideology, viii, 5, 11, 19, 60, 61, 83, 85–86, 130, 145, 147

Scalia, Antonin, 44
School busing cases. *See* Racial desegregation cases
Scope of study, 17–18
Second-order diversity, 139
Segregation cases. *See* Racial desegregation cases
Senate role in judicial confirmation, 1–2, 87, 141–44
"Senatorial courtesy," 6
Seventh Circuit, 108
Sex discrimination cases, 26f, 30–31, 117, 145
Sexual harassment cases, 31–32
Sexually explicit speech. *See* Obscenity
Sixth Circuit: and breakdown of reciprocity, 67; and lack of dampening effect, 63; party effect vs. panel effect of, 111
Social comparison as explanation for group polarization, 74–75
Souter, David, 44
Sovereign immunity cases. *See* Eleventh Amendment cases
Standing to sue, cases on, 11, 12, 49t, 53–54, 61, 145
Statutory interpretation, 132
Stevens, John Paul, 44
Supreme Court: aftermath of major opinions of, 150; appointee adhering to ideology of appointing president, 130; and creation of binding precedent, 83; mix of cases heard by, 124; more conservative